Anthony Trollope

D0332893

SUTTON POCKET BIOGRAPHIES

Series Editor C.S. Nicholls

Highly readable brief lives of those who have played a significant part in history, and whose contributions still influence contemporary culture.

SUTTON POCKET BIOGRAPHIES

Anthony Trollope

GRAHAM HANDLEY

SUTTON PUBLISHING

First published in 1999 by
Sutton Publishing Limited · Phoenix Mill
Thrupp · Stroud · Gloucestershire · GL5 2BU

British Library Cataloguing in Publication Data
A catalogue record for this book is available from the British Library

ISBN 0 7509 2270-2

Typeset in 13/18 pt Perpetua
Typesetting and origination by
Sutton Publishing Limited
Printed in Great Britain by
Bath Press, Bath

To Lily Butcher, with love

CONTENTS

LIST OF
ILLUSTRATIONS

ACKNOWLEDGEMENTS & FURTHER READING

Anyone writing on Anthony Trollope today has full resources on which to draw. In the last decade or so, four distinguished and detailed biographies (by Robert Super, Richard Mullen, N. John Hall and Victoria Glendinning) have been published, each in their vivid particularities enhancing our appreciation and understanding of a major Victorian writer. I acknowledge here the benefits I derived from these in the period 1989–1993, and have referred back to notes made on them at the time of reading. I must similarly record my debt to N. John Hall's exemplary edition of *The Letters of Anthony Trollope* (1983). Peter Rooke helped me with the choice of illustrations. I am grateful to my editors, Jaqueline Mitchell and Helen Gray. My greatest personal debt is to John Letts OBE, chairman of the Trollope Society, who read my manuscript and made a number of stimulating suggestions, most of which have been incorporated. The Trollope Society is flourishing here and in America, its aim of having all Trollope's fiction in print as cased editions virtually accomplished. Scholarship and criticism matches Trollope's own writing span, while Richard Mullen's *The Penguin Companion to Trollope* (1996) and the *Oxford Reader's Companion to Trollope* (1999), to which a number of contemporary Trollopians have contributed, reflect the density of interest in his work. Television productions of *The Pallisers* and *The Barchester Chronicles* in the 1970s and 1980s kept this much-loved writer in the public eye, and I recently discovered a video of one of Trollope's best stories, 'Malachi's Cove' (1987). Cassettes and readings on radio of the major novels occur regularly. I hope that the short biography which follows will contribute towards the picture of the man and his writings for readers approaching Trollope for the first time or renewing acquaintance with him. There is a very rich verbal territory to explore, and I use the metaphor deliberately to echo Trollope's lifelong propensity for physical and mental journeyings.

CHRONOLOGY

(Publication dates given below are those of the first book issue of each of Trollope's works. Serial/part publications are not listed).

1815	**24 April.** Born 16 Keppel Street, London; family afterwards moves to Harrow
1823	At Harrow School
1825–7	Private school at Sunbury
1827	At Winchester College
1831	Returns to Harrow again
1834	Family flight to Bruges; does six weeks as usher in school in Brussels; in November appointed junior clerk in Post Office, London
1835	Father dies
1840	Seriously ill in summer
1841	Postal Surveyor's clerk, Banagher, Ireland
1844	**11 June.** Marries Rose Heseltine
1846	Henry Merivale Trollope born
1847	Frederic James Anthony Trollope born; *The Macdermots of Ballycloran*
1848	*The Kellys and the O'Kellys*
1850	*La Vendee*
1851	Seconded to England on postal duties

1853	Returns to Ireland as Northern District surveyor
1855	Settles at Donnybrook, Dublin; *The Warden*
1857	*Barchester Towers; The Three Clerks*
1858	*Dr Thorne*; postal mission to Middle East (January); postal mission to the West Indies (November)
1859	*The Bertrams; The West Indies and the Spanish Main*; buys Waltham House (November); appointed Postal Surveyor, Eastern District of England
1860	*Castle Richmond*; meets Kate Field in Florence
1861	*Tales of All Countries* (1st series); *Framley Parsonage*; visits America
1862	Elected to Garrick Club (April); *North America; Orley Farm*
1863	*Tales of All Countries* (2nd series); *Rachel Ray*; death of Frances Trollope
1864	*The Small House at Allington; Can You Forgive Her?*
1865	*Miss Mackenzie*; hunting, travelling, clerical sketches published
1866	*The Belton Estate*
1867	*Nina Balatka* (published anonymously); *The Last Chronicle of Barset; The Claverings; Lotta Schmidt and Other Stories* (October); retires from Post Office, forgoing pension
1868	*Linda Tressel* (published anonymously); three-month trip to America; loses election as

Chronology

Liberal candidate for Beverley, Yorkshire

1869	*Phineas Finn*; *He Knew He was Right*
1870	*The Vicar of Bullhampton*; *An Editor's Tales*; *The Commentaries of Caesar*
1871	*Sir Harry Hotspur of Humblethwaite*; *Ralph the Heir*; leaves for eighteen-month tour of Australia and New Zealand in May
1872	*The Golden Lion of Granpere*; *Shilly-Shally* in West End Theatre; returns home via New York; lodging in Holles Street
1873	Takes house in Montagu Square; *Australia and New Zealand*; *The Eustace Diamonds*
1874	*Phineas Redux*; *Lady Anna*; *Harry Heathcote of Gangoil*
1875	*The Way We Live Now*; goes to sort out Fred's affairs in Mortray; visits Ceylon (begins *An Autobiography*)
1876	*The Prime Minister*
1877	*The American Senator*; goes to South Africa end of June
1878	*South Africa*; June–July in Iceland; *Is He Popenjoy?*
1879	*Thackeray*; *An Eye for An Eye*; *John Caldigate*; *Cousin Henry*
1880	*The Duke's Children*; *The Life of Cicero*; moves to South Harting near Petersfield (July)
1881	*Dr Wortle's School*; *Ayala's Angel*
1882	*The Fixed Period*; *Palmerston*; *Kept in the Dark*; *Marion Fay*; two visits to Ireland; moves to London (October); has a stroke

INTRODUCTION

At the beginning of November 1834 a young man presented himself at the Post Office in St-Martin's-le-Grand, London, having been recommended, through the patronage of a friend of his mother's, for a junior clerkship. He has said that his handwriting then and there was scrutinized and condemned, he was told that he would be further examined the following day on another example which he was required to provide, and that he would also be given a test in arithmetic, something he greatly feared since he did not know his tables. That evening he dutifully made a clean copy of an extract from Gibbon's *The History of the Decline and Fall of the Roman Empire*, took it in the next day, and never heard of it again. According to his own account, the dreaded arithmetic examination was also forgotten. He was confirmed in his junior clerkship, paid initially £90 per annum, and soon exasperated his employers by his lateness, inefficiency and inattention to his duties.

He seemed likely to lose his job, and was
frequently in debt.

The young man was Anthony Trollope: he would
write, between 1845 and his death in 1882, forty-
seven novels, forty-two stories, four major travel
books and a minor one descriptive of a select group's
jaunt to Iceland, a miscellany of articles, reviews,
lectures, sketches and casual pieces, brief lives of
men as various as Thackeray and Lord Palmerston,
and a massive life of his beloved Roman author
Cicero. His activities and interests became numerous.
He would rise to a high position in the Post Office,
revitalize many of the postal systems of his time both
within Great Britain and Ireland and elsewhere, and
travel widely in the world: he would appropriate the
concept, and recommend the inauguration, of the
pillar-box, that mini-memorial to his professional
dedication which may be set beside the maxi-
memorial of his fiction.

Having retired from the Post Office in October
1867, he would stand as a Liberal candidate for the
Yorkshire constituency of Beverley in the following
year, when his leader Gladstone had a comfortable
victory. He was not elected and came bottom of the
poll: the constituency was disfranchised for

corruption (he himself was blameless), and for the next twelve years or so he subjected the political scene to an ironic and telling scrutiny in his fiction, examined the state of society, continued his travels, wrote almost without pause (one brief novel was even futuristic) and lived his clubman-cum-committee-man life in tandem with what undoubtedly was a happy domesticity, about which he hardly ever talked. His letters however bear testimony to it and reveal, too, his concern and devotion to his two sons in his attempts to promote their respective careers.

Late on he gave up one of the loves of his life, hunting, but his zest in all directions was undiminished. His son, Henry, in the preface to his father's *An Autobiography* (written in 1875 but with instructions to Henry not to publish it until after his death) tells us that: 'Every day, until his last illness, my father continued his work. He would not otherwise have been happy. He demanded from himself less than he had done ten years previously, but his daily task was always done'.[1] Death came six weeks after a stroke in December 1882: typically, Trollope had one novel which was unfinished, one was running in a magazine as a serial at the time of his death, and his desk yielded up its posthumous publications. Some argue that *An Autobiography*, that fascinating mixture of reticence and revelation published in 1883, gave a downward tilt to his reputation, his description of writing 250 words to order every fifteen minutes after being awakened in the early hours of each morning taking the gloss off the idea of romantic inspiration.

Anthony Trollope's reputation has more than recovered itself in the twentieth century, particularly in the latter half, where his civilized and urbane writing, deliciously and sometimes comically romantic in the Barchester sequence, having touches of darkness as he grew older but always irradiated by compassion, humanity and the sheer delight in narrative, has endeared itself to many. Almost everything he wrote is now in print, and he has a devoted following. But his is not merely a literary voice from the past: the man is as interesting and compelling as his books, his story in so many ways mirroring the Victorian period itself. Although he probably agreed with his great friend George Eliot that the real biography of an author's life is in the words he or she wrote – and his own *An Autobiography* is remarkable for its careful omissions though not without considered evaluations of his own writings – he lived his professional and public and his guarded private lives to the full. In the words of the first of his recent biographers, Trollope's is 'the story of the life of an interesting, versatile, significant man'.[2] It is a reasonably modest claim but a just one. Trollope, after beginnings which promised little and produced less, came to practicality, maturity and something more than talent, hence his interest for us today.

TRIALS AND TRIBULATIONS

Anthony Trollope was born on 24 April 1815 at 16 Keppel Street, Bloomsbury, London, the fourth son of a sparsely-practising barrister, Thomas Anthony Trollope, and his wife Frances (*née* Milton). His eldest brother, Thomas Adolphus, was born in 1810, and became a literary man, writing novels, travel and history. Two other brothers, Henry (born 1811) and Arthur (born 1812), died young, the first in 1824 and the second in 1834 some weeks after Anthony's appointment in the Post Office. Emily, born in 1818, survived until 1836. Her death was perhaps the most traumatic for Anthony. He wrote feelingly to Tom in February of that year, 'Poor Emily breathed her last this morning. She died without any pain, and without a struggle.'[1] The fourth member of the family to die from the scourge of consumption was Cecilia (born 1817). She had married Anthony's friend and colleague, John Tilley, and survived until April 1849 before succumbing at the age of thirty-two.

Anthony's father was a melancholy man of extreme moods, his mother a vivacious woman of great fortitude and industry, as she was soon to demonstrate. Some short time after Anthony's birth the family moved to Harrow-on-the-Hill where Thomas Anthony had unwisely leased some farmland, and by 1823 Anthony was attending Harrow School as a day-boy. The plan was that he should go on from there to Winchester, his father's old school, and from there to Oxford (Tom and Henry had been sent to Winchester in 1820/21). The early pages of *An Autobiography* reflect just how conscious Anthony was of his hobbledehoy image, his poor clothes, the various petty incidents of this phase of his schooldays, as he saw them later, and other more serious marks of denigration which emphasized his sense of isolation. The boys who lived at home were often snubbed and bullied. Even if we allow for some exaggeration in this recall of his early life, the tone of bitterness, largely absent from his adult life, is unmistakable.

Mr Trollope had expectations, having calculated that he would be left money by a rich relative, Adolphus Meetkeerke. But these fell through when Meetkeerke remarried at the age of sixty-four, his wife being much younger than he was.

Soon the shunting which was to disrupt Anthony's development began. In 1825 he was transferred to a private school in Sunbury, and from there to Winchester College two years later where, according to his own account in *An Autobiography*, he was regularly flogged by his brother Tom as part of his daily discipline and further endured the then spartan conditions of school life. By now the family was in dire financial straits. Influenced by a friend, Frances Wright, who had founded a Utopian community at Nashoba in Tennessee with the object of freeing the slaves, Frances Trollope sailed for America in November 1827. Her son Henry and two daughters accompanied her, as did an artist friend, Auguste Hervieu, a member of the Trollope household at Harrow. He was devoted to her, and continued to be (he later illustrated her books) and would have been of practical help with the community idea in the capacity of teaching. However, Frances apparently spent less than a fortnight at Nashoba, where the community had a high incidence of disease and was in a largely disorganized state, before she left for Cincinnati.

The initial disaster of Nashoba was compounded by Frances' sheer impracticality in business. She set up a kind of superstore (known later to many as 'Trollope's Folly'), in which she intended to have 'a variety of shops and boutiques on the main floor, with a refreshment hall and gallery for paintings; on the next a ballroom and concert hall . . .'.[2] In 1828 her husband and eldest son sailed to join her, leaving Anthony behind. He was at Winchester at this time, and felt somewhat forsaken. Frances hoped to sell goods which her husband had purchased for the venture, but failure was absolute. In 1829 Tom and Mr Trollope returned, followed by Henry, and because of the lack of funds and increasing debts Anthony had to leave Winchester in 1830. He returned to Harrow at the beginning of the following year, and resumed his daily walks to school and back to the decaying farmhouse. His memories stress the fact that he was dirty and slovenly, but there is little doubt that he acquired the lasting effects of an interest in the Latin classics which were to give him so much pleasure throughout life. Ten years before he wrote of this time of personal suffering in *An Autobiography* he had sung the praises of the public schools for installing courage and integrity in their pupils.

Frances Trollope, like her son Anthony after her, found travel the stimulant she needed despite the weight of adversities. She arrived back from America at the beginning of August 1831, and scarcely seven months later had published *The Domestic Manners of the Americans*, which became a bestseller. It angered many Americans, so much so that the name 'Trollope' became equated with unfair criticism of their way of life, but it found an appreciative reading public in England. She made enough money to settle the most pressing debts, though the family fortunes could hardly be completely retrieved or set on a firm footing. She became a literary lion, and followed her initial success by writing a wide range of books. Her next was called *The Refugee in America*. Her subjects included popular travel, works of social concern (*Michael Armstrong, the Factory Boy*) and she of course contributed to the current vogue for romances. Despite her son's later strictures on their quality, her novels exhibit a remarkable variety. Her husband meanwhile was beginning the laborious task of compiling his *Encyclopedia Ecclesiastica*, his temper, indigestion, headaches and the general malaise of moods certainly exacerbated by the misprescription of drugs.

Anthony may have felt left out even after his mother's return, but he must have admired her incredible achievements and self-discipline: she became a role-model at least in part for his own future practice. She nursed her ailing husband, wrote her books, socialized, and spent. As Anthony later wrote, 'She was at her table at four in the morning, and had finished her work before the world had begun to be aroused.'[3] By contrast his father continued to decline, having nothing of his wife's taste for what Anthony calls 'joy'. 'The touch of his hand seemed to create failure' and 'His life as I knew it was one long tragedy'[4] are his son's poignant glosses on a failed life. But the ambitious nature of his father's literary project may have influenced his son to entertain the idea some time later of writing a history of world literature. Meanwhile Anthony himself had little time for joy, though on one occasion he and Tom apparently walked from Harrow to Vauxhall Gardens to see the amusements there, and then walked home again in the small hours of the following morning.

In April 1834 the family were forced to leave the country because of their debts. Mrs Trollope was already on the continent gathering information for her next book, and Anthony had to drive his father to London to catch the Ostend boat. Lord Northwich, their landlord, had seized their property and possessions because of their debts: they literally scuttled out of the back door as the debt collectors arrived at the front. They went to Bruges, Anthony and his sister Cecilia arriving in May, and Henry joined them there. He was already in the later stages of consumption. Anthony in fact had a short taste of teaching, acting as classics' usher at a school in Brussels for a period of about six weeks. He has left on record, again with some bitterness between the lines, the fact that he had failed to get into Oxford or Cambridge, though when he left Harrow at the age of nineteen he was in fact near the top of the school. He never forgave the Headmaster, Dr Butler, for castigating his dirtiness in the street much earlier in his school career and casting doubt on whether this really was a Harrow boy: Anthony knew he knew who he was, for 'he was in the habit of flogging me constantly'.[5]

But in October 1834 the clerical vacancy in the Post Office arose. The son of Sir Francis Freeling, secretary to the Post Office in London, was married to a friend of Frances Trollope, and through the good offices of this friend an interview was granted to Anthony. His appointment was confirmed early in November. On 23 December his brother Henry died. The new era in his life had opened sadly and things were to get progressively worse on both personal and professional levels as the nineteen-year-old Anthony insecurely began his career.

He and his fellow clerks had the primary task of copying documents, generally letters, their hours being from ten until four. Eighteen months after Anthony's appointment Freeling died and was succeeded by Lieutenant-Colonel Maberly, who was pretty soon at odds with his junior clerk. But Anthony did have his leisure, and has given some account of the long walks he enjoyed with his friends Henry Merivale (this was a lifelong attachment) and Walter Awdry, touring the countryside and vowing never to spend more than five shillings a day. Anthony read, he had ambitions to write, he played cards and, of course, he got into debt. One amusing incident is recounted in *An Autobiography* which was later to be recycled in *The Three Clerks* (1857). Anthony tells how he was embarrassed in front of his colleagues by the arrival of a woman in the office who upbraided him for not saying when he was going to marry her daughter, the latter having been convinced (which Trollope was not) that he had proposed to her. In the novel Charley Tudor, who has many marks of identity with the young Anthony Trollope, is confronted at his work by Mrs Davis, landlady of the Cat and Whistle (the pub much frequented by Charley). Charley has become romantically involved with her barmaid, Norah Geraghty:

'And, Mr Tudor, what are you a-going to do about that poor girl there?' said Mrs Davis, as soon as she found herself in the passage, and saw that Charley was comfortably settled with his back against the wall.

'She may go to Hong-Kong for me.' That is what Charley should have said. But he did not say it. He had neither the sternness of heart nor the moral courage to enable him to do so. He was very anxious, it is true, to get altogether quit of Norah Geraghty; but his present immediate care was confined to a desire of getting Mrs Davis out of the office.

'Do!' said Charley. 'Oh, I don't know; I'll come and settle something some of these days; let me see when – say next Tuesday.'

'Settle something,' said Mrs Davis. 'If you are an honest man, as I take you, there is only one thing to settle; when do you mean to marry her?'[6]

Meanwhile Anthony's father died on 23 October 1835, and Mrs Trollope took a house at Hadley near Barnet early in 1836, bringing the now terminally ill Emily with her. Anthony came down from London to stay with them from time to time. Again there is a link with *The Three Clerks* where the young Katie Woodward, whom Charley Tudor really loves, goes into a decline which seems to be fatal. She survives, for fiction can be made softer than life.

With typical resilience Mrs Trollope was in Vienna by the summer, collecting material for her forthcoming study of *Vienna and the Austrians*. Tom was appointed to a teaching post at King Edward's Grammar School, Birmingham, and Anthony muddled on in London. He was in trouble in 1838 for failing to produce a copy of a document, his pay was held over for a week as a result, and he also had to stay behind after office hours to do extra work. There was some brightening of the atmosphere when one of Anthony's fellow clerks, John Tilley, later to rise to the heights of executive authority in the Post Office (and to have some rivalry with Anthony), married his last surviving sister Cecilia in February 1839. He had just been appointed as a district surveyor for the Post Office in Northern England. The house at Hadley was given up in 1838, Mrs Trollope moved temporarily to London and then fell in love with the Lake District. She researched *Michael Armstrong, the Factory Boy*, took a house at Penrith and then, towards the end of 1839, went to Paris with Anthony to give him a holiday. After his return he became ill, and from May to September 1840 he was on sick leave, later visiting his mother and the Tilleys in Cumberland.

Anthony's appraisal of his mother in *An Autobiography* was criticized by his brother Tom after his death. It is a curious mixture of pride in her courage and criticism of her writing and personality. He said that everything with her was 'an affair of the heart', and added of her bestselling book that 'The Americans were to her rough, uncouth, and vulgar, – and she told them so. Those communistic and social ideas, which had been so pretty in a drawing-room, were scattered to the winds.'[7] Her fame encouraged her natural tendency towards social climbing, and her son Anthony was hardly dissimilar from her in this respect.

In addition to his postal work, Anthony had acted for his mother with publishers in London, a practice from which he was to benefit later. By 1841 his salary had risen to £180 per annum, but his reputation had not risen with it. When the position of Postal Surveyor's clerk came up in Banagher, Ireland, Anthony decided to apply for it. The salary was £100, but the travel and subsistence expenses were such that he could hope to earn at least £300. His application was successful, and he has suggested that Maberly was only too glad to see him go and that, had he not done so, he might not have survived in the Post Office much longer. He cleared his debts and provided for his initial expenses by borrowing £200 from a relative. He has left one amusing account of his relations with Maberly which testifies to his feelings of frustration during his office life. A letter placed there by the clerk, Trollope, was missing from Maberly's desk:

When the letter was missed I was sent for, and there I found the Colonel much moved about his letter . . .

'The letter has been taken,' said the Colonel, turning to me angrily, 'and, by G——! there has been nobody in the room but you and I.' As he spoke he thundered his fist down upon the table. 'Then,' said I, 'by G——! you have taken it.' And I also thundered my fist down; but, accidentally, not upon the table. There was there a standing movable desk, at which, I presume, it was the Colonel's habit to write, and on this movable desk was a large bottle full of ink. My fist unfortunately came on the desk, and the ink at once flew up, covering the Colonel's face and shirt-front. Then it was a sight to see that senior clerk, as he seized a quire of blotting-paper, and rushed to the aid of his superior officer, striving to mop up the ink; and a sight also to see the Colonel, in his agony, hit out right through the blotting-paper at that senior clerk's unoffending stomach. At that moment there came in the Colonel's private secretary, with the letter and the money, and I was desired to go back to my own room. This was an incident not much in my favour, though I do not know that it did me special harm.[8]

T W O

A REAL CHANGE

Trollope arrived in Ireland in mid-September 1841, the base for his operations being established at Banagher on the Shannon, a central location. He had the daily travelling allowance referred to above, and he was soon riding the length and breadth of the country, which he came to love. He turned the screw on those who were inefficient and established his own authority in the outlying places, for instance dealing summarily with a defaulting postmaster on Galway Bay.

Hitherto trapped behind a desk and what he called 'this wretched life' of debt, passing degradation and frustration, Anthony now surfaced into an unclerical and free-ranging life which gave him the impetus for success. It *made* him, for in many ways he was able to become his own man, a travelling man physically but, one senses from his own words, a travelling man imaginatively as well. Even as a boy he had gone about 'with some castle in the air firmly built within my mind' and had chosen 'to live in a world altogether outside the world of my own material life'.[1]

By July/August 1842 he was in Kingstown, a seaside place close to Dublin. Here he met the Rotherham bank manager, Edward Heseltine, and his daughters. He married one of them, Rose, on 11 June 1844, in Rotherham, naming that day as being 'the commencement of my better life'.[2] Typical of his reticence though is his laconic observation some two or three pages later that, 'My marriage was like the marriage of other people, and of no special interest to any one except my wife and me.'[3] He was soon introduced to the sport of fox-hunting which was to become the passion of his life whenever he had leisure; socially too his life expanded, and he visited his old Harrow friend, William Gregory, at Coole Park, a place later indelibly associated through Gregory's second wife with the poet W. B. Yeats. Trollope's first two novels were set in Ireland, as was his final uncompleted one. He saw the famine of 1846–7 at first hand, and later got into print in the *Examiner*, then edited by Dickens' friend John Forster, by supporting the government measures in Ireland which had been so condemned by radicals in London.

Above all initially, he made his professional mark, and he also set up in his own mind a databank on which he could draw to sustain the imaginative life which was so essential to him. Always the ambition to be a novelist was present. In 1843 he tentatively began his first novel, based on his observation of a distinctive old house at Drumsna in Leitrim. It set his imagination working, and in that first novel, *The Macdermots of Ballycloran*, he describes it. After his marriage to Rose he was appointed clerk for the Southern District of Ireland in August 1844, and moved to Clonmel in Tipperary, which became his next base. In 1846 and 1847 sons were born to this socially rising couple, Henry in March 1846 and Frederic in September 1847. Trollope was instrumentally responsible for improvements in the postal services, helping to initiate the movement of mail from coaches and Bianconi's cars to the emergent and extending railways in Ireland. His own peregrinations continued, and by 1848 he had moved house to County Cork.

The Macdermots of Ballycloran, once largely forgotten but now accorded due recognition, was published in 1847. It is notable for its compelling local associations, a command of dialect and the incidence of violence which culminates in murder and hanging, and, perhaps above all, for Trollope's understanding of Ireland and the nature of its sufferings. It was followed by *The Kellys and the O'Kellys* (1848), again containing violence and brutality. It was a commercial failure, and Trollope's publisher Colburn felt that he could not advise him to continue writing novels.

Paralleling these early fictions were Trollope's professional commitments. Sometimes these provided him with material which could be adapted or employed as a basis for expansion. There is the instance of his using a marked coin to trap a postal thief: this led to his having to attend court and be cross-examined in 1849. Courtroom scenes, particularly those involving the eccentric but powerfully individualized lawyer Chaffanbrass, stand out in *The Three Clerks*, *Orley Farm* and *Phineas Redux*, and are a feature of Trollope's dramatic narrative. His need to write was certainly stimulated by the Irish experience on a number of levels. Reference has been made earlier to the letters which appeared in the *Examiner* in response to Sidney Godolphin's letters to *The Times* which were critical of the government. Trollope's replies

(signed AT) began in August 1849 and described the
real state of Ireland as he saw it.

In that year his sister Cecilia died (her husband
John Tilley had been promoted assistant secretary
to the Post Office in 1848). Almost immured to
tragedy, Trollope continued to work and write,
beginning his only historical novel *La Vendee*
(published in 1850) which is set during the
excesses of the French Revolution. It deals with the
revolt of the people of that district on the Loire
against the repressive government in Paris. Trollope
undertook detailed research (he read among much
else Archibald Alison's ten-volume account of the
French Revolutionary period), combining fictional
characters of his own making with originals who
were developed under his own hand. When he read
the novel years later Trollope felt that it had some
merit. In Adolphe Denot, obsessive and manic, we
find the first of a line of characters in his fiction
whose imbalance is felt and presented with truth
and intensity.

Trollope's first three novels failed and a play
written at about this time, *The Noble Jilt*, was also
rejected by his theatre-manager friend George
Bartley, though Trollope much later cannibalized the

plot into the first of his political novels, *Can You Forgive Her?* (1864) and referred self-mockingly to this dramatic failure in *The Eustace Diamonds* (1873). But Trollope as postal official enjoyed an increasingly upward curve. He became friendly with the celebrated Bianconi, whose cars still often carried the mail in Ireland, for although trains were used the cars had not yet been completely superseded, and there was considerable advice and help forthcoming over the most efficient routes to be followed.

In 1851 Anthony was seconded to England: interestingly he mentions in a letter to Tom the Great Exhibition of that year, adding that his wife has a piece of work in it, identified by Hall as an embroidered screen which was given a medal.[4] Trollope's brief was to undertake broad postal reform and tighten efficiency in the south-western counties. The reorganization of the delivery of letters in the rural areas was his abiding concern, and he asserted that it was his ambition to establish rural letter carriers over every part of the country. He prescribed that no postman should walk more than 16 miles a day, and he himself walked or rode over the routes to ensure accuracy and practicality of delivery. He averaged about 40 miles a day himself on horseback. In the ten years since he had arrived in Ireland he had been completely transformed: the reluctant clerk was now a man of considerable importance in his profession. But if Ireland made him in that professional sense, England was to make him in a career which was to run in tandem with his work for the next fifteen years. His own words are eloquent here:

> In the course of the job I visited Salisbury, and whilst wandering there one midsummer evening round the purlieus of the cathedral I conceived the story of *The Warden*, – from whence came that series of novels of which Barchester, with its bishops, deans, and archdeacon, was the central site.[5]

Although thought out between 1852 and 1853, *The Warden* was not published until 1855. It featured the lovable and suffering warden, Mr Harding, and his angry and bossy son-in-law Archdeacon Grantly. It launched the series by which its author was to be best known and loved, *Barchester Towers* following it two years later. Trollope the postal official reorganized the postal services of the counties while Trollope the novelist created a county of his own in which the power struggles of High and Low Church were seen in comic and sometimes acidic interaction, supplemented by romantic situations of moving particularity.

As the county of his imagination took shape the counties of fact were combed and integrated. Trollope claimed to have visited the majority of houses in Devon and Cornwall and a large number in Somerset and Dorset, as well as taking in five of the central counties and much of South Wales. R.H. Super has commented on Trollope's infinite capacity for getting the best out of himself and doing the best for himself both in terms of his profession and the developing nature of his leisure:

> His zeal for the service was reinforced by the wish to augment his income with as large an allowance for mileage as possible, and in the winter he could arrange his routes to take in all the most interesting hunts of the region.[6]

This organized channelling of his energies, different but of mutual independence and importance, is the characteristic which stands out in Trollope's ways of life. His professional dedication is clearly seen – and evident in the permanent sense – as a result of his being sent to the Channel Islands towards the end of 1851, where he quickly reorganized routes, again making his priorities the efficient use of time and labour, and then proceeded to advocate a positive solution which would help those who were some distance from a post office in St Helier. He thought that it might be positively useful to have letter boxes attached to walls at about a height of 5 ft wherever practicable so that the public could deposit their letters.[7] It was not completely original, Trollope admitting that he had got the idea from France where such boxes were apparently found on roadside posts.[8] The pillar-box was born: it is the first signal and abiding instance of Trollope's professional practicality. In essence it has yet to be superseded. Within a few years such boxes had spread all over the United Kingdom. Trollope could not forbear a casual mention of what had been done nearly twenty years later in *He Knew He Was Right* (1869) where the eccentric Jemima Stanbury registers her mistrust of this change.

After a continental holiday with Rose in 1854 (this was to become a feature of their lives, with visits to Tom Trollope and his mother, now in Florence), Trollope returned to Ireland first as

Acting Surveyor then as Surveyor for the Northern Disrict in 1854, initially in Belfast, and soon moved to set up home at Donnybrook in Dublin at about the time *The Warden* was published. His salary was now £700 a year plus a generous travelling and expense allowance which enabled him to live more comfortably, and he had achieved senior status within the postal service. Meanwhile he resisted the attempts to introduce competitive examinations for entry into the Civil Service as advocated in the Northcote-Trevelyan report of 1855, even including caricatures of the initiators (as Sir Gregory Hardlines and Sir Warwick Westend) in *The Three Clerks* (1857). The novel also contains a parody of supposed examination practice. Interestingly, Charles Dickens' attack on bureaucracy in the Civil Service, which he lampooned as the Circumlocution Office in *Little Dorrit* (published 1855–7) apparently drew a reply from Trollope which has unfortunately been lost.

In 1855 *The Warden* was published. Trollope's trenchant comment later was, 'The pecuniary success was not great. Indeed, as regarded remuneration for the time, stone-breaking would have done better.'[9] But in it he was intent on redressing abuses, like the possession by the Church of money to be used for charitable purposes which was in fact being siphoned into the pockets of Church dignitiaries (he had a notorious contemporary case in mind). He also castigated abuse by the press (the *Jupiter* is the masking name for *The Times* in the novel) of people who were the innocent recipients. Another area of critical comment included Dickens, who is called 'Mr Popular Sentiment'.

The Warden made no waves, but reflected Trollope's early satirical zeal, and he followed it with *The New Zealander*, which was rejected by his publisher Longmans and had to wait until 1972 when it was edited and published by N. John Hall. (The title is taken from Macaulay's prophetic vision of a New Zealander surveying a future, ruined London.) It is a radical examination of various aspects of contemporary society which Trollope particularly disliked, newspapers and evangelicals, for example, and other favoured hates which, as Hall rightly notes, were to feature thematically in many of Trollope's novels. Longman's reader was scathing in his report. He also read the next in the emergent sequence, *Barchester Towers* (1857). This introduced the prelatess Mrs Proudie and her ally then enemy Mr Slope, integrating into their interaction the lovable warden and the angrier archdeacon. That crippled Cleopatra, the man-eating Madeline Neroni *née* Stanhope, embarrassed Joseph Cauvin, the Longman's reader who had condemned *The New Zealander*, by her 'love-making' with Slope: he considered her 'a great blot on the work'.[10]

As well as reflecting the High–Low Church struggles of the time, Trollope had now emerged as a successful comic-romantic writer. He immediately began *The Three Clerks* which, as we have seen, mirrored another area of contentious contemporary debate, its official and office bureaucracy seen in the Weights and Measures and the Internal Navigation respectively. There was some lifting from the unpublished *The New Zealander* and a running emphasis on the corrupt nature of aspects of society, a theme which Trollope was to explore more fully in the momentous *The Way We Live Now* some eighteen years later.

THREE

HOME AND AWAY

In the early autumn of 1857 Anthony and Rose visited Tom and the now ageing and feeble Frances Trollope in Florence. Her final novel, *Fashionable Life; or Paris and London*, had been published in 1856: she lived on until 1863, and although Anthony was dismissive of her abilities as a writer ('But she was neither clear-sighted nor accurate; and in her attempts to describe morals, manners, and even facts, was unable to avoid the pitfalls of exaggeration'),[1] there is little doubt that she was an important influence on him. The need to travel (now that he had the means he could travel at leisure) grew increasingly upon him. Momentous new directions in his professional life were beginning to appear, and these would further feed into his other professional life, that of a writer. He fixed up a portable writing-desk which he used in railway carriages and on board ship, and sent his work in pencil to Rose for transcription. She was effectively his first editor, a role she occupied for much of their married life.

In January 1858 he left England to go to Egypt and the Middle East on postal business, visiting the Holy Land and taking in Malta, Gibraltar and Spain on the way home. This mission – to facilitate the carrying of mail through Egypt by railway instead of the hitherto dated transportation in bags and boxes (Trollope feared that mailbags could be easily cut open with a knife) – also included the aim of a treaty with Egypt. This treaty would allow for the transfer of mail between Alexandria or Suez to or from India and Australia. The negotiations were completed by 23 February. Typically Trollope had worked on *Dr Thorne* (third in the Barset sequence) throughout his travels, finishing it on 31 March and beginning *The Bertrams* (which has a Middle Eastern sequence) promptly afterwards. *Dr Thorne* – Anthony acknowledged his brother Tom's hand in the plot – occasioned an affectionate letter to Rose at the beginning of February 1858, in which he urges her to take care in her reading of what he has sent, 'and also alter any words which seem to be too often repeated'.[2] Rose's editorial responsibilities were obviously considerable, and this letter reflects how much Anthony owed to her through her practical dedication to his writing. R.H. Super has admirably expressed the pattern that was developing: 'His missions abroad produced his travel books and articles, as well as a series of short stories based on his observations of life in foreign countries, and gave substance for some of his novels.'[3]

Two stories from this trip also give evidence of his whimsical humour, the first being 'An Unprotected Female at the Pyramids' (first published in 1860) while the second 'A Ride Across Palestine' (first published in 1861) is a daring (for the time) sequence narrated by a male traveller of his journey with a companion who turns out later to be a woman disguised as a man. She was escaping from her uncle, does not join in the bathing in the Jordan (how could she?) but there are teasing episodes when, for example, the narrator wakes to find his head in 'her' lap. It was strong stuff, and was rejected by Trollope's new publisher George Smith, who was squeamish about the sexual implications.

Trollope pressed on, all experience providing him with ready-to-hand material. By now his travelling was more by train than on horseback, and in the summer and early autumn of 1858 he was operating in his official capacity in the northern counties and Scotland. In November he left on a postal mission for the West Indies, *The Bertrams* being published in March 1859 while he was away. The West Indian brief was his most important yet, for it involved the wholesale reorganization of the local postal system and encountered an attendant local opposition. He dealt with the postmen's walks as he had done in Ireland and England, surveyed shipping details and the transport of mail, engaged with the Spaniards to reduce their charges for forwarding it, effected economies and straightened out procedures in small and large compass. Effectively, he was able to travel freely if often uncomfortably throughout the Caribbean. His achievements were exemplary, and he saved the Post Office many thousands of pounds.

Naturally, almost reflexively, he had agreed to write a book about his experiences. *The West Indies and the Spanish Main* was published in October 1859. Trollope was later to write of it with some degree of pride, not without justification. Among its many enchantments are his account of the penal settlement in Bermuda (later there was a story –

'Aaron Trow' – derived from this location, a terrifying, escaped-convict near-rape sequence), his evaluation of the slave situation, and the enunciation of some racial views which would be found appalling today. Trollope is forthright, honest, unequivocal, the man of his time recording the facts of his time as he saw them. He was also enabled, via a Spanish passport for which he paid sixteen shillings in Kingston, to mock his own appearance. His body was rather more flatteringly referred to in Spanish than he was used to, his eyes were given as 'azure', his baldness was ignored, while the word 'poblada' (bushy) was used to define his distinctive physical attribute: 'If I have any personal vanity, it is wrapped up in my beard. It is a fine, manly article of dandyism, that wears well in all climates, and does not cost much, even when new.'[4]

He had his first taste of America (a tremendous stimulant) on the way home, and in July 1859 he submitted his report. His most important recommendation was the establishing of Jamaica rather than St Thomas as the centre for mail in the region. Already the measure of his success had reached the first of its peaks. He was appointed Surveyor of the Eastern Counties of England

(Essex, Cambridge, Huntingdon, Suffolk and Norfolk, together with parts of Hertfordshire and Bedfordshire), which meant removal from Donnybrook. He leased a large house, Waltham House, at Waltham Cross on the Hertfordshire–Essex borders, spending £1,000 on improvements. It was a mere 12 miles from Shoreditch station in London by train, and sufficiently contiguous to the Essex hunt to make his professional and leisure life compatible. He was now within reach of those levels of society which he had probably always felt were his natural aim. In the next few years he was accepted into them as of right, though his own hard work was responsible for the achievement.

The immediately specific nature of this social ascent must have given him unalloyed delight. He was invited by his idol, the novelist William Makepeace Thackeray, celebrated primarily for his *Vanity Fair* (1848), to contribute a novel to the new monthly magazine, the *Cornhill*, which the publishing tycoon George Smith was launching in January 1860. Trollope had already written in, offering five stories, but this was recognition indeed. Despite the fact that he was already at work on an Irish novel (*Castle Richmond*) Trollope changed direction, returned imaginatively, romantically, expressively to Barchester, and began his first serial, *Framley Parsonage*, fourth in the Barsetshire series. It took pride of place in the *Cornhill*'s first issue, and the novelist Mrs Gaskell probably crystallized a majority reaction to it when she wrote to George Smith, 'I wish Mr Trollope would go on writing Framley Parsonage for ever'.[5] The illustrator, who got on well with Trollope after their first brush (Trollope was often caricatured for his abrasiveness), was the thirty-one-year-old John Everett Millais (1829–96), a major Pre-Raphaelite painter. He and Trollope were to become lifelong friends, and he would illustrate *Orley Farm* and *The Small House at Allington*.

By the beginning of 1860 Trollope was the man of the hour. He was shortly to cement his status, at least in his own mind, by getting himself onto the club circuit which constituted a kind of social recognition. He published the Irish novel *Castle Richmond* in 1860, and again visited his brother Tom and his mother in Florence in the autumn of that year, meeting the Brownings while he was there (Elizabeth reportedly found his beard 'extraordinary'). And, more significantly, at the age of forty-five, he met Kate Field, an attractive, intelligent and shortly-to-be an active feminist. She was American and twenty-two, just half his age. That he loved her in some way is apparent, that he continued to do so over the years is certain, but it seems very unlikely that there was any sexual relationship. Rose corresponded with her, and both husband and wife saw her on a number of occasions both in America and on her visits to London. Trollope's own account is delicately, tactfully but emotionally put from his hindsight position in 1875:

> There is a woman, of whom not to speak in a work purporting to be a memoir of my own life would be to omit all allusion to one of the chief pleasures which has graced my later years. . . . She is a ray of light to me, from which I can always strike a spark by thinking of her. I do not know that I should please her or do any good by naming her. But not to allude to her in these pages would amount almost to a falsehood. I could not write truly of myself without saying that such a friend had been vouchsafed to me. I trust she may live to read the words I have now written, and to wipe away a tear as she thinks of my feelings while I write them.[6]

Kate was actress, poet, lecturer, writer: she never married. Her relationship with Trollope has intrigued commentators over the years: her own writing records their friendship in easy, balanced and respectful terms. From time to time she invited him to comment on her poetry and fiction, and there is certainly every evidence in his letters that he did so directly and honestly without emotional embarrassment

With the publication of *Framley Parsonage* in the *Cornhill* Trollope reached a wider public than hitherto. The first issue of the magazine sold in excess of 100,000 copies, and although circulation fell it was the leading periodical of the time, providing space for high-quality fiction, with George Eliot, Thackeray, Mrs Stowe and others among its early contributors. But success and the new house, with its walled garden, strawberry beds, lined bookroom and, we are told, adjacent rooms for mail workers, only stimulated Trollope to increased activity. Awkward and independent as ever, he fell out with Rowland Hill, effectively head of the Post Office, over the question of whether promotion should be by merit or seniority in the service. Trollope held the view that the passing over of men whose long service entitled them to expect reward was bad for morale.

Waltham House was both his retreat and his pride. He and Rose enjoyed the leisure of entertaining their friends, whose overnight stays were common. She was responsible for the cows, the roses and the strawberries. The summer evenings on the lawn frequently found Anthony indulging his cigars and good conversation. London was enhanced, as it would be for so many of his fictional characters, by the acquisition of clubland status: in April 1861 Trollope was elected to the Cosmopolitan Club. It was the first of his chosen few.

He had helped G.H. Lewes (George Eliot's partner) to get his son Charles into the Post Office and, some time later, doubtless remembering his own early waywardness and indolence, told Lewes that Charles was doing badly and needed to apply himself, which he did. He defended himself to Thackeray against the charge that one of his (Trollope's) stories ('Mrs General Talboys') was indecent, and in March 1861 indulged himself in a piece of whimsy by writing to a Miss Sankey, telling her that his 'excellent wife' is still alive but that it was always necessary to anticipate the future by being prepared for any eventualities. 'Should anything happen to her, will you supply her place, – as soon as the proper period for decent mourning is over.'[7]

Trollope managed to get himself sent to America at a crucial time, though he was nearly prevented from obtaining his seven months' leave by the opposition of Rowland Hill. He left in August 1861 (naturally he had contracted to write a travel book about his visit, thus reinvoking his mother's practice some thirty years earlier), and he and Rose arrived in Boston in early September. The internecine strife between North and South had already started with the clash at Bull Run in July, and Trollope shortly afterwards wrote to Kate Field deploring this indicator of the bloodshed to come. He was graphically describing what he saw within days of his arrival. He met celebrities like Emerson and Lowell (the latter found him loud and overbearing), and absorbed feelingly the full degradation of war. He commented on modes of travel (he liked the sleeping cars, but he did not like overheated rooms). He found travelling on the horse-drawn street cars in New York somewhat embarrassing, noting that aggressive women eye-blackmailed men to give up their seats to them. In Boston he heard a lecture by the abolitionist Wendell Phillips, but felt that there was too much lecturing by far. He visited Niagara and has left a superb account of the experience: he made time to stay in Canada, evaluate its constitution, conjecture that it might become independent of England later, and climb Owl's Head mountain with Rose, an experience which they both enjoyed. He also visited woodcutters, and was delighted to find that they had books to read.

In America situations were grist for the fictional mill. Sleigh-driving in Boston provided him with the idea for one of his stories ('Miss Ophelia Gledd'), but factual history was at hand too. With the removal of the Confederate officers from the *Trent* by the Northern navy, Trollope was an on-the-spot eyewitness to an international crisis between the North and England. He looked back and went back too, visiting his mother's old and now decayed bazaar in Cincinnati. He found it 'under the dominion of a quack doctor on one side, and of a college of rights-of-women female medical professors on the other'.[8] But England was much in his mind with the news of the Prince Consort's tragic death in December 1861.

North America, a massive and rambling compilation, reflected the breadth and range of Trollope's experiences and views: in some ways – perhaps many – he felt that America was of overwhelming credit to the mother country she had left. Typically, he was greatly moved at seeing families split by the conflict, one of his stories, 'The Two Generals' reflecting the brother–brother division. According to Richard Mullen, when he addressed an audience on his return to England he asserted that slavery degraded the slave-owner more than the enslaved,[9] and he deplored the idea of conscription.

Trollope arrived back in England in March 1862 and quickly published *North America*, while *Orley Farm* (with illustrations by Millais) continued its part issue. The novel is an impressive and moving analysis of deception, inheritance, forgery and the law (Chaffanbrass again in evidence), with the bold technical trick of maintaining suspense in the reader despite having revealed the truth, but it also contains a typical Trollopian indulgence, here a plot pivot: the hunting scene he so loved to introduce is functional, for the accident suffered by Felix Graham facilitates his romance with Madeline Staveley. Trollope also published a fictional skit on advertising (*The Struggles of Brown, Jones and Robinson: By One of the Firm*) which, though it featured in the *Cornhill*, merely reflects his reflex and often uncritical tendency to overproduction.

FAME AND CONSIDERABLE FORTUNE

Trollope was now at the height of his powers, part of the literary and social élite as well as of the professionally elevated. He began to devote his time to the Royal Literary Fund, which was designed to give help to needy authors and their families. It became one of his major interests (his letters testify to his conscientious labours and his warm heart), and his life membership was a sympathetic identification with his fellow authors. He was elected to the Garrick Club in April 1862 (two years later almost to the day he was to make it into the Athenaeum), later playing whist there in the afternoons and succeeding Thackeray as a member of the committee. For the Christmas number of the magazine *Good Words* (January 1863)

he wrote a story called 'The Widow's Mite', which
shows his continuing obsession with the American
Civil War. It describes a woman's act of sacrifice for
the cotton weavers in Lancashire who had been
rendered unemployed by the conflict. He published
another volume of stories the same year and a novel
called *Rachel Ray* which exhibits something of his
anti-evangelical stance, though his friend the
novelist George Eliot wrote of his heroine, 'Rachel
herself is a sweet maidenly figure & her poor
mother's spiritual confusions are excellently
observed'.[1] Eliot added of his writings, 'the books
are filled with belief in goodness without the
slightest tinge of maudlin'.

On 6 October 1863 his mother died. He
remembered her struggles on the family's behalf (he
and Tom were the only surviving children) and
wrote, much moved, to a friend who had written an
obituary of her, thanking him for his kindness and
tasteful treatment.

The Barchester sequence continued with *The
Small House at Allington* (serialized 1862–4, with
illustrations by Millais). The betrayal of Lily Dale by
Adolphus Crosbie, the love Johnny Eames bears her
and her (kindly) rejection of him, plus Eames'

giving Crosbie a black eye at Paddington station (reported as a 'thrashing') ensured a captive readership then as now. Again, one feels there is a cunning fictionalizing of the past or even the present: Sir Raffle Buffle, Eames' superior at the Income Tax Office, is a caricature perhaps taken mockingly from life, and Eames, like Charley Tudor before him, might have something of the younger Trollope, even to the extent of near entanglement with the predatory Amelia Roper.

In March 1863 Trollope's niece, Florence Bland, came to live with Anthony and Rose: she would prove to be an invaluable aid to him in later years as she transcribed his words, his late manuscripts being written in her clear hand. By now, as one might expect, part of his status arose from his various social activities, and at the annual dinner of the Royal Literary Fund in May 1863 he responded to the toast 'The Writers of Fiction' with an eloquent defence of the novel because its moral and spiritual qualities were in effect supportive of society in the best sense. He also upset Sir Rowland Hill further by lecturing on the Civil Service and advocating freedom of action and political views for its employees.

On Christmas Eve 1863 Thackeray died, and Trollope attended the funeral six days later at Kensal Green Cemetery. Fifteen years or so on Trollope wrote a monograph on his revered friend. In the first, and biographical, section of Trollope's short book he says: 'To give some immediate pleasure was the great delight of his life, – a sovereign to a schoolboy, gloves to a girl, a dinner to a man, a compliment to a woman. His charity was overflowing. His generosity excessive.'[2] He then proceeds to give an instance of this generosity, occasioned by a needy friend in urgent want of cash. Thackeray agreed to put up £1,000 as a loan if Trollope would provide the other half necessary to relieve his friend. He did. Trollope's own generosity, of heart and spirit, is never in doubt.

In 1864 Sir Rowland Hill resigned from the Post Office. Trollope, despite their considerable differences of opinion and practice over the years, wrote him a generous letter paying tribute to his dedicated work in improving the postal services. John Tilley replaced him, and Frank Scudamore replaced Tilley as assistant secretary. Trollope himself (with his own belief in promotion by seniority) undoubtedly wanted the position: there was an

Anthony Trollope in his fifties, a typical study of him at about the time he resigned from the Post Office and sought to enter politics. (© *Popperfoto*)

Frances Trollope, Anthony's indomitable mother, painted by Auguste Hervieu shortly after Fanny's success with the *Domestic Manners of the Americans* (1832). (*By courtesy of the National Portrait Gallery, London*)

The house at Hadley, near Barnet, where Anthony often stayed with his mother (1836–8) and where his sister Emily (aged seventeen) died in February 1836. (*By courtesy of Teresa Ransom*)

Tom Trollope, Anthony's brother, with his first wife Theodosia, their daughter Bice (Beatrice) and the ageing Frances Trollope at their home in Florence about 1860. Anthony and Rose visited there regularly. (*By courtesy of Victoria Glendinning*)

General Post Office (right), St Martin's le Grand, 1852, where Anthony began work as a
clerk in November 1834; lithograph by T. Picken after drawing by W. Simpson. (*Guildhall
Library, Corporation of London, UK / Bridgeman Art Library, London / New York*)

Anthony rose to high office and was instrumental in initiating improvements in the service
both at home and overseas. This shows the first despatch of mailbags through pneumatic
tubes in 1863. (© *Illustrated London News*)

Drawing of Anthony by the celebrated cartoonist 'Spy', which appeared in *Vanity Fair* in 1873, an indication of Trollope's status. (*By courtesy of the National Portrait Gallery, London*)

The first cover, by George Housman Thomas, from Anthony's final novel in the famous sequence about Barsetshire, *The Last Chronicle of Barset*. The novel appeared in weekly parts from December 1866 until July 1867. C.190e.16. (*By permission of the British Library*)

The cover for Part XI of *The Way We Live Now*, Anthony's lacerating attack on corrupt practices in contemporary society. The novel was issued in twenty monthly parts, from February 1874 until September 1875. December 1874 issue; 0.11350d.7. (*By permission of the British Library*)

The frontispiece for Anthony's novel *Orley Farm* (1861–2) by the celebrated Pre-Raphaelite artist, John Everett Millais, who became a friend. C.190e.15. (*By permission of the British Library*)

This composite photograph (1876) places Anthony with his great contemporaries, including W.M. Thackeray (*front, left*) and Charles Dickens (*front, right*), something he whimsically appreciated. (*By courtesy of the National Portrait Gallery, London*)

initial falling out with Tilley, who offered him a postal mission to the Middle East and India, which he declined. But the rupture was soon healed.

Immediate compensations were certainly there in Trollope's election to the Athenaeum and his elevation on to the committee of the Royal Literary Fund where he remained for the rest of his life. Perhaps too he covertly recognized that events were already conspiring to nudge him away from the world of postal politics and into the real world of political (and fictional) action. The first novel in his great political sequence, *Can You Forgive Her?* belongs to 1864, and there is a deliberate overlap here in terms of characters with *The Small House at Allington*, almost as if Trollope was introducing his next sequence while taking a long farewell of the previous one. Hablot K. Browne (known as 'Phiz'), Dickens' illustrator from *Pickwick Papers* onwards, was employed to illustrate the monthly publication of the novel but he was removed before the end of it, his techniques perhaps too dated to vivify the text. Henry James, reviewing the novel in the *Nation*, responded to the interrogative of the title by observing, a touch unkindly, 'Of course we can, and forget her too, for that matter'.[3] But *Can You Forgive*

Her? is in many ways the first modern English novel. Despite its exposure of corruption (a recurring later Trollopian theme), it also contains signals of one of the directions in which its author was being pulled. This is seen in his observation of the entrance to the House of Commons that, 'It is the only gate before which I have ever stood filled with envy, – sorrowing to think that my steps might never pass under it.'[4]

There followed a number of hunting sketches, travelling sketches, a series of essays later in book form called *Clergymen of the Church of England*, and a novel called *Miss Mackenzie*, which again had its share of evangelical satire as well as an unlikely heroine. It also has a scene which reveals a particular Trollopian bias, peripheral to the plot but central to his current reactions: this is a charity bazaar (for negro soldiers' orphans in the American Civil War) which finds Trollope mocking society snobbery, the name-dropping opportunities of being associated with something 'charitable'.

His own activities were in fact on the edge of even greater expansion. A group of influential literary and publishing men had convened themselves late in 1864 with the object of issuing a new periodical: following the initial financial success of the *Cornhill*, periodicals were an inviting prospect at the time. As a result, the *Fortnightly Review* was founded, Trollope investing £1,000 in the venture. Launched in 1865, it had G.H. Lewes, a close friend of Trollope, as editor, while Trollope himself contributed a novel, *The Belton Estate*, to it as well as airing in it his views on the Civil Service and other topics of contemporary interest. Trollope was also involved with George Smith (of *Cornhill* fame) in producing an evening newspaper, the *Pall Mall Gazette*. That too came out in 1865, and Trollope wrote essays and sketches for it, as well as an article on 'Bazaars for Charity'.[5] He felt he was at the centre of cultural informed commitment, his life expanding in the one sphere while it was contracting, almost inevitably, in the profession to which he had devoted half his days. He loved to have his own verbal platform, partaking of leisured observation though stimulatingly controversial, but he did not appreciate being asked to cover the May series of Evangelical meetings at Exeter Hall.

His critical and debating self revelled in social activities, but at about this time his corpulence began to bother him. He came under the influence of a self-taught dietician who, a hundred years before the weight-conscious obsessions of the mid-twentieth century, discovered that a high protein intake combined with low sugar and starch promoted physical health through decreasing girth. Trollope adopted the plan, the improvement in his appearance being duly noted by his friend George Eliot. Though the weight returned later in his life, he paid his own tribute to William Banting in his novel *The Fixed Period* (1882), where he is described as 'that great Banting who has preserved us all so completely from the horrors of obesity'.[6]

In April 1865 Tom's wife Theodosia died, and Anthony and Rose took in Tom's daughter Bice for a time. She was taught by Frances Ternan, later to marry Tom and become a novelist in her own right as well as the biographer of Frances Trollope. She was the sister of Dickens' mistress Nellie Ternan. Meanwhile Anthony's postal assignments still occurred regularly. He went to Glasgow to speed up the passage of mail to and from London, then holidayed in Germany and Austria in the late summer of 1865, saying goodbye to his son Frederic in Vienna as he set out for Australia with high hopes of making a living as a sheep farmer. Prague made a particular impact on Trollope, and provided him with the setting for his (initially) anonymous short novel *Nina Balatka*, while Nuremberg gave him a contrasting location for its companion piece, *Linda Tressel*. There have been various interpretations of his need to take on the challenge of anonymous publication at this stage: it is not so much a mid-life crisis as the need to prove himself anew, and perhaps even a symptom of his determination to undertake something different, a characteristic always present in his make-up. Nina's story was that of a Catholic in love with a Jew with the inevitable complications, but although the location is seen and felt the characters hardly come alive under the author's pen. One feels the restlessness beneath the print, almost as if Trollope is searching for his own identity in the process of creating others. Socially, his own identity seems full and clear. Through Lord Houghton, editor of Keats and like himself voluntary toiler for the Royal Literary Fund, he met Tennyson, dined with Browning, and was now firmly in the foreground of the literary men of his day. Professionally, he reorganized the London District Postal systems in 1866, but turned down an invitation from John Tilley to take over the area as Surveyor.

It seems likely that he had already decided on the move he was going to make, but before that he left Barsetshire. *The Last Chronicle of Barset* marked his farewell to the 'beloved county', and the neatness and moving qualities of this rounding-off cannot be overemphasized. The warden Mr Harding dies in peaceful and venerated old age, the archdeacon comes to accept his son's forthcoming marriage to the daughter of an impoverished clergyman falsely suspected of stealing a cheque, and in the characterization of that clergyman, the Revd Josiah Crawley, Trollope scales (and plumbs) new levels of psychological insight into the mind and emotions of that demented man. The novel reflects how completely Trollope lived with his characters, how integral they were to his life, as real as living people, how he had walked about 'crying at their grief, laughing at their absurdities, and thoroughly enjoying their joy'.[7] His anecdote about Mrs Proudie, one of his outstanding creations, shows the quality of his identification with his creatures. He tells how one morning in the Athenaeum he heard two clergymen talking of his work:

> The gravamen of their complaint lay in the fact that I reintroduced the same characters so often! 'Here,'

said one, 'is that archdeacon whom we have had in every novel he has ever written.' 'And here,' said the other, 'is the old duke whom he has talked about till everybody is tired of him. If I could not invent new characters, I would not write novels at all.' Then one of them fell foul of Mrs Proudie. It was impossible for me not to hear their words, and almost impossible to hear them and be quiet. I got up, and standing between them, I acknowledged myself to be the culprit. 'As to Mrs Proudie,' I said, 'I will go home and kill her before the week is over.' And so I did . . . I have sometimes regretted the deed, so great was my delight in writing about Mrs Proudie, so thorough was my knowledge of all the little shades of her character.[8]

For Trollope, telling stories was his reflex mode of entering that other, imaginative life. The anecdote indeed may be fiction rather than fact: it has the stamp of a kind of theatrical utility. Trollope dramatized *The Last Chronicle*, perhaps his greatest novel, as *Did He Steal It?* without success. He was fascinated by the theatre: in the last fifteen years of his life he annotated and commented on more than 250 Elizabethan and Jacobean plays,[9] and one feels that he would have liked to contribute something to drama in his own right. He was to, though unwittingly, before many years were out.

His writing continued apace: he looked back to Ireland (one story, 'Father Giles of Ballymoy', dates from this time, and is a humorous and self-mocking piece with autobiographical derivations), and he began to write *Phineas Finn*, the second of his political novels, which introduces an Irish hero with political ambitions. It is as if he is almost subliminally charting his own course, though more than a year would pass before things came to a climax. He and Rose attended the wedding of his brother Tom and Frances Terhan in the autumn of 1866. Back in England Trollope found that his old friend G.H. Lewes was resigning as editor of the *Fortnightly*. The young John Morley was installed in his place, with Trollope playing the role of consultant.

Another change was at hand, and had been carefully prepared for. Trollope became editor of *St Paul's* magazine, to which he contributed *Phineas Finn* and which he ran for over two-and-a-half years. Another continental holiday resulted in a short novel called *The Golden Lion of Granpere*, which would not be published until five years later. And then, in October 1867, he resigned from the Post

Office. He was fifty-two years old, and took the step knowing that he would forgo his pension since he had not reached the statutory age of sixty. One of his colleagues, Edmund Yates, who had stirred up the Garrick Club affair some ten years earlier which caused the estrangement between Thackeray and Dickens, described Trollope as bullying, loud and coarse, but admitted that he probably had a kind heart. At the end of October 1867 a farewell dinner was held for Trollope to mark his retirement.

He was becoming increasingly drawn towards practical politics, and *St Paul's* dealt with the contemporary concerns which enabled him to air his opinions and evaluations of a variety of subjects, though he sometimes found the work oppressive. He watched debates from the gallery of the House of Commons, a dual emphasis as ever apparent – fodder for his fiction and practical knowledge for what might be a newly opening career. It was almost as if he were an apprentice MP. Like his creature, Phineas Finn, he opposed one of the main issues of the time, the use of the secret ballot when votes were cast. He could see the chief figures of the day like Gladstone and Disraeli in action, and could use them as models for his own fictional equivalents (of course his creations were of his own making, as he rightly claimed), called Mr Gresham and Mr Daubeny. These and others have an impressive individuality of their own in a context dear to their creator.

As always, there were various factual and fictional irons in the fire. He began to write a powerful novel which was unpolitical: it was initially called *Mrs Trevelyan*, but was later changed to *He Knew He Was Right* (finished in June 1868, and published in thirty-two sixpenny parts between 1868 and 1869). Still spurred by the challenge of different activities and interests, in April 1868 he went to America on a postal mission (in his retirement!), spending a miserable time there, failing to reach a conclusive agreement, finding the heat of Washington unbearable and making jokey doggerel out of it for Kate Field ('Sumner alone he might have stood/But not the Summer weather', a reference to the controversial American senator, Charles Sumner).[10] He was also concerned to bring about a copyright agreement between England and America (he had lost out consistently on the issuing or reprinting of his own books there) but this too failed. As he arrived in New York, he made a point of seeing Dickens, who was just leaving. And of course Kate Field had the benefit of his advice on her writing. Of one story, called 'Love and War', he observed that it was lacking in plot and was too self-centred. Touching the second fault first, it is always dangerous to write from the point of "I" . . . . The old way, "Once upon a time", with slight modifications, is the best way of telling a story.'[11] Did he ever stop working, thinking, writing, judging, commenting, being committed to whatever was at hand? His letters show a consistency of application over a variety of areas which is unremitting.

FIVE

POLITICS AND AFTER

After his return to England Trollope realized that he had missed out on the jockeying for political position and preference because of his trip to the States. Having hoped to be selected for a convenient Essex seat, he now discovered that he was to be nominated as one of two Liberal candidates for the town of Beverley in Yorkshire. He was later to write:

> I have always thought that to sit in the British Parliament should be the highest object of ambition to every educated Englishman. I do not by this mean to suggest that every educated Englishman should set before himself a seat in Parliament as a probable or even a possible career; but that the man in Parliament has reached a higher position than the man out, – that to serve one's country without pay is the grandest work that a man can do, – that of all studies the study

of politics is the one in which a man may make himself most useful to his fellow-creatures . . .[1]

This was written in 1875, and shows Trollope after the chastening experience of electoral defeat looking back from what he called his 'conservative–liberal' position. And even in the political novels, where corruption is exposed and opportunist lobbying frequently overcomes principle, Trollope is still sure of the system, one feels, still sure despite the knowledge that his radical insights have exposed the parliamentary game for what it is. Trollope uses the image himself when defining his own political theory, remarking on 'the intriguers, the clever conjurers, to whom politics is simply such a game as is billiards or rackets, only played with greater results'.[2] Trollope never had the chance 'to confine himself and conform himself, to be satisfied with doing a little bit of a little thing at a time',[3] despite his vast experience on Post Office committees.

The Beverley experience was more than chastening. Canvassing meant being at the whim not just of the public but of the agents who managed him. Typical of Trollope, hindsight lent humour to the view – 'At night, every night I had to speak somewhere, – which was bad: and to listen to the speaking of others, – which was much worse.'[4] With education for all as the main plank in his political platform, Trollope was certainly showing his moral responsibility, the calibre of his radical views. Interestingly, the Education Act of 1870 which established the national provision of elementary education was only two years away, and was carried through by Trollope's friend and fellow-whist player, W.E. Forster.

Trollope got fewer votes than the other three candidates and paid, according to his own account, some £400 for the venture, saw the borough of Beverley disfranchised, and returned to fiction and travel, later adapting the factual events to a fictional account in *Ralph the Heir* (1871). Trollope was cleared of any taint of corruption by the committee which sat in judgment on the borough, and felt that he had stood out for principle and integrity. The year 1869 saw the issue of *Phineas Finn* and *He Knew He Was Right* in book form after their respective serial and part publications, the second having as its major focus the manic jealous husband, Louis Trevelyan. Others have noted his morbid tendencies as perhaps deriving from Trollope's father, and Robert Kennedy, in *Phineas Finn* and *Phineas Redux*, the jealous husband of Lady Laura, is also deranged. In both novels Trollope, through the study of marriage, is appraising the lot of the unhappily married woman who has no practical or moral redress to alleviate her situation. It reflects Trollope's many-sidedness, and it is a curious paradox that the man who could mock aspects of contemporary feminism was, above all, aware of the 'disabilities' – his word in a later context – suffered by women in the untender trap of enforced subjugation.

In the following year Trollope went even further, engaging with the dubious fictional subject (for the time) of prostitution in *The Vicar of Bullhampton*. Uniquely for Trollope, he wrote a preface to the novel for this aspect of its content, saying of the girl Carrie Brattle that:

> I have endeavoured to endow her with qualities that may create sympathy, and I have brought her back at last from degradation at least to decency. I have not married her to a wealthy lover, and I have endeavoured to explain that though there was possible to her a way out of perdition, still things could not be with her as they would have been had she not fallen. [5]

This reflects another aspect of Trollope's humanity and his moral radicalism: he was not afraid to discuss, in his fictional world, issues with which the Victorian reading public was concerned, though its attitudes smacked of hypocrisy. Trollope's stance here is even more explicit in *An Autobiography*, where he refers to 'we' closing our door upon erring daughters. 'But for our erring sons we find pardon easily enough.'[6]

A morbid short novel with Cumberland locations, *Sir Harry Hotspur of Humblethwaite*, followed, but practical eventualities such as setting up his son Henry as a partner in the publishing firm of Chapman & Hall (reputedly at a cost of £10,000) showed his warm concern for his children. Sadly, Frederic and Henry both failed in the sense that their separate careers came to nothing, Henry leaving the firm in 1873 while Frederic had to be bailed out later by his father from the Mortray farm in New South Wales. Meanwhile *St Paul's* was failing financially too, and Trollope left in July. He had published *An Editor's Tales* (1870), a collection distinguished by 'The Spotted Dog', a story of an impoverished scholar reduced to hack work and completely undermined by an alcoholic wife.

Trollope could turn his hand to anything which interested him. He never read or lectured to the extent that Dickens or Thackeray did on their celebrated tours, but his own offering 'On English Prose Fiction as a Rational Amusement' shows him setting out his stall, the wares of which would be more fully displayed in *An Autobiography* in his comments on contemporary novelists. Meanwhile, in January 1870 selected provincial towns had the benefit of his views on fiction and his particular love for Jane Austen's work. He was moved to another departure from his practising norm, though again it is not surprising if one knows his interests. He did *Caesar's Commentaries* for John Blackwood's *Ancient Classics for English Readers* series, drawing modern parallels between Caesar's acquisition of territories and the growth of the British Empire in India, for example. The book shows his channelled energy, the quality of his imagination – old study freshened by new zest and his constant search for new areas to explore or old areas to mine for the excitement and relevance of their yield.

Meanwhile, on 9 June 1870 Dickens died, five years to the day after he had been involved in the nightmarish rail accident at Staplehurst. Trollope, still writing for *St Paul's*, contributed an article on 'The Inimitable' in which he said that Dickens believed 'entirely in the people, writing for them, speaking for them, and always desirous to take their part as against some undescribed and indiscernible tyrant'.[7] It was the right language at the right time, but wider issues soon arose: the Franco–Prussian War broke out in July, and for Anthony and Rose the usual continental tour running into the autumn was impossible. Trollope switched into alternative reflex action: writing in the space of a month a searing story with an Irish setting, *An Eye for An Eye*. It involved murder, tragedy, insanity. Truly, as one critic has put it, much of Trollope's later fiction reflects a 'changing world'.[8] He continued, however, to see his many friends, meeting Turgenev when he visited Lewes and George Eliot, and then in 1871 he began one of his masterpieces, a fringe novel in the political series, *The Eustace Diamonds*. Set in London and Scotland, it is rich in contemporary reference (he even mentions the Underground at Swiss Cottage, which opened in 1868), and has some comic policemen as part of the sensation plot, Trollope undoubtedly having in mind the recent successes in this area of his friend Wilkie

Collins. The heroine derives from Thackeray's Becky Sharp in *Vanity Fair*, but is strongly and viciously individualized in her own right. According to T. H. Escott, Disraeli observed to Trollope, 'I have long known, Mr Trollope, your churchmen and churchwomen; may I congratulate you on the same happy lightness of touch in the portrait of your new adventuress?'[9] This is how Lizzie Eustace appeared to a discerning eye.

It soon became necessary to think of giving up Waltham House. It had been so convenient because of his Post Office work and for what Trollope himself referred to as 'suburban hospitalities',[10] but it was also far from weatherproof and its upkeep was expensive. Trollope and his wife had been very happy there, but having decided to go to Australia to see Fred it seemed extravagant to keep it on, and in any case the idea of settling in London on their return had now taken hold. They sailed on 24 May 1871 with the intention of being abroad for eighteen months – 'So there was a packing up, with many tears, and consultations as to what should be saved out of the things we loved.'[11] The tone is low key, typical of the emotional reticence which characterizes so much of *An Autobiography*, but beneath it lies the twelve years of established security and attendant status, of hosting friends and guests, of a way of life that was to change as Trollope and Rose got older.

With that indefatigable energy which characterized his lifestyle – which was also his workstyle – Trollope began *Lady Anna* on their first day at sea and finished it before they docked in Australia. Richard Mullen has pointed out the almost casual relevance of the novel's subject-matter to their travelling context.[12] The novel deals with the love of Lady Anna for the son of a radical tailor who has helped her mother to prove her right to the title: at the end we are told that the young couple 'were bound for Sydney. . . . They would at any rate learn something of the new world that was springing up, and he would then be able to judge whether he would best serve the purpose that he had at heart by remaining there or by returning to England'.[13] Before setting out himself Trollope contracted to write a travel-book on Australia and also to supply the *Daily Telegraph* with a series of letters from the region.

He traversed the continent, analysed state legislatures, produced statistics (as he would do later of his earnings per book in *An Autobiography*) and also statements which are so typical of his independent stance. He felt that the Australian aborigines should be allowed to peacefully disappear, an idea unpalatable to us today. The Trollopes' stay with Fred led later to a short novel, *Harry Heathcote of Gangoil*, in which Trollope acknowledged that the hero was modelled on his son. Fred actually organized a kangaroo hunt for his father, who later managed to have an accident in the more conventional hunting with the Melbourne staghounds. Trollope registered sheep-shearing graphically and visited gold mines and the Chudleigh stalactite caves, as well as the low-life districts of Ballarat.

In July 1872 he sailed for New Zealand, falling in love with the Maoris and their traditions but feeling that they could not survive. He regarded them as superior to the Australian aborigines in every way, and amusingly records bathing in the hot pool near a village and being patted on the back by Maori girls by way of encouragement. The incredible and often punishing itinerary continued; meanwhile back in London Charles Reade adapted *Ralph the Heir* (Trollope's novel based on his political experience at Beverley) for the West End theatre under the title of *Shilly-Shally*. It ran for a month. Trollope was furious and felt betrayed. He wrote to George Smith: 'It is monstrous that I should be made to appear as a writer of plays without my own permission, – or that I should be coerced into a literary partnership with any man.'[14] He and Rose returned towards the end of 1872 via San Francisco and New York, and the massive travelogue was completed in January 1873.

After their return they lived initially in Holles Street near Oxford Street, which placed Trollope within easy reach of his clubs and many friends and publishers. Naturally, he took up again where he had left off with the Essex hunt. *The Eustace Diamonds* was published in book form in this year, and soon Trollope was reading John Forster's *Life of Dickens* (1872–74), and adopting in a letter a somewhat different emphasis from his public statement of nearly three years earlier:

Dickens was no hero; he was a powerful, clever, humorous, and, in many respects, wise man; – very ignorant, and thick-skinned, who had taught himself to be his own God, and to believe himself to be a sufficient God for all who came near him.[15]

At about this time Trollope confided to Lewes that Henry had fallen for 'a woman of the town'[16] (such was the euphemistic phrasing of the time). Henry was sent to Australia to see Frederic and presumably get over it. Anthony and Rose settled in Montagu Square, and he contracted to write what was to be one of his greatest novels, *The Way We Live Now*. The celebrated cartoonist 'Spy' drew him for the magazine *Vanity Fair*, he had Kate Field to dine with Wilkie Collins, who had already conditioned himself to find her adorable (and saw much of her afterwards), while Mark Twain on another occasion appreciated Trollope's perfect English, something of a contrast, one feels, with the loud and overbearing Trollope reported by other observers.

The political sequence continued with *Phineas Redux* (serialised between 1873 and 1874), literally 'Phineas Brought Back'. Again the sensational element of the time is apparent here in the plot, which harnessed itself to the current vogue by having Phineas tried for the murder of the repugnant Mr Bonteen. Chaffanbrass is recalled from fictional retirement and given great verbal play, but the focus is once more on the sufferings of a woman, Lady Laura Kennedy, wife of the mad

Robert. Phineas is largely saved by the efforts of Madame Max Goesler, whom he later marries. Trollope, sometimes accused of racism and anti-semitism, makes this eastern European woman of dubious background one of the most attractive, compelling and independent of his heroines.

But *The Way We Live Now*, with its action set virtually contemporaneously in 1872, shows Trollope's expansion not only into a darker mode (though the novel certainly has its comic sequences), but also into a comprehensive indictment. His own words, written not long after the publication of the novel in book form (1875) following its part issue, are relevant here. Commenting on what he calls the rise of 'dishonesty' and its acceptance in the upper levels of society, he says:

> Instigated, I say, by some such reflections as these, I sat down in my new house to write *The Way We Live Now*. And as I had ventured to take the whip of the satirist into my hand, I went beyond the iniquities of the great speculator who robs everybody, and made an onslaught also on other vices, – on the intrigues of girls who want to get married, on the luxury of young men who prefer to remain single, and on the

puffing propensities of authors who desire to cheat the public into buying their volumes.[17]

It is a modest claim and almost diminishes the scope of the novel, which is not limited to satire: it is a studied and sustained exposure of rampant commercialism and all the attendant corruptions which buttress and extend its nature. The title has passed into our language, and has been cited in its full morally ironic emphasis to define and describe our own times in the latter half of the twentieth century.

In the book, Roger Carbury represents the old values, but the main thrusts are at a dessicated aristocracy, outsider influence and takeover, swindling speculation with paper money, together with gambling on a personal and public scale. It also tilts at British social prejudice and the idea that money is power even in a morally aware society. Trollope is using the public models of his time and earlier, like the railway king George Hudson and the recent suicide of another con man, John Sadleir. He includes contemporary detail suitably transliterated, such as the Shah of Persia's visit to England in 1873, which becomes the Emperor of China's dinner given by the arch-swindler Melmotte. The latter's triumph in getting himself elected as Conservative member for Westminster is another Trollopian swipe at Disraeli (are politics totally corrupt too?). An unpublic original is Father Barham, the ubiquitous Catholic priest who even penetrates the Melmotte house in his quest for money to support the Faith. When Trollope was at Waltham House he too was pestered by such a person, recording that he had succeeded in making himself intolerable. As for Lady Carbury, intent on literary fame, with her systematic chatting-up of influential editors, perhaps she derives partly from Frances Trollope. Although she is presented satirically the portrait is not without compassion.

SIX

THE WAYS HE LIVED THEN

Trollope's own life was still filled with action, though he was becoming increasingly aware of the penalties of age: he feared, for example, that the loss of hearing in one ear was permanent. He put himself about with his usual dedication, helping to get pensions for the families of two deceased editors of *Punch*, Mark Lemon and Shirley Brooks. The Cremation Society was formed in 1874, with Trollope as an ardent supporter, so much so that he was to use the idea of cremation in his futuristic novel, *The Fixed Period*, some eight years later. In 1874 he began to write *The Prime Minister*, the penultimate novel in the Palliser series, with its central focus on the public life of his ideal politician, Plantagenet Palliser, and on his private life with Lady Glencora. But dishonesty as a theme would not go away and, in the person of the ambitious but devious Ferdinand Lopez, Trollope continued his assault on financial malpractice. Melmotte's suicide by cyanide in *The Way We Live Now* is here matched by the public suicide of Lopez at the Tenway (railway) Junction, a climactic scene which has some parallels with Anna's death in *Anna Karenina*. Tolstoy's masterpiece was coming out in 1873–77 (*The Prime Minister* was issued in eight monthly parts between November 1875 and June 1876).

But such was Frederic's financial position that Trollope was moved to go to Australia again. He arrived in May 1875, cleared up debts of more than £4,000, and began *The American Senator*. Again he arranged to write letters about his travels, providing twenty for the *Liverpool Mercury* covering his visits to Ceylon, Fiji, the South Seas and back via San Francisco: he gave some account of the Stock Exchange there, which was on the edge of violence ('Paris is more than six times as large as San Francisco; but the fury at San Francisco is even more demoniac than in Paris').[1]

He also began *An Autobiography*. P. D. Edwards and others have noticed the importance of 'An' in the title, since this implies facets rather than fullness. He left instructions to his son Henry that the book should not be published until after his death. Deliberately selective, it is nevertheless wonderfully readable, full of interest in terms of Trollope's views of literature, politics, his professional career and the nature of his own writing. He tells of his daily habits of composition, compares the art of writing books with the craft of the cobbler, spells out his preferences for Jane Austen and Thackeray as against Dickens, and perhaps lulls the reader by the persuasiveness of his hindsight to accept everything he says as being accurate and true. It is not – he sometimes got things wrong – but there is no doubting the honesty of his intentions. And, as if finally to lay to rest the myth that authorship is romantic, he includes an account of his earnings for each book he wrote.

Particularly important is the view of this failed politician of the ideal politician he created: Plantagenet Palliser is a man, albeit dull, who is a politician by hereditary right, a man of complete integrity (Trollope's own word here is 'scrupulous'). He has the highest moral aims in public life and a wife who, denied political franchise, is effectively his domestic prime minister. Again we note how real these characters were to their creator, how they developed under his hand. He wrote:

> I think that Plantagenet Palliser, Duke of Omnium, is a perfect gentleman. If he be not, then am I unable to describe a gentleman. She is by no means a perfect lady; but if she be not all over a woman, then am I not able to describe a woman. I do not think it probable that my name will remain among those who in the next century will be known as the writers of English prose fiction; – but if it does, that permanence of success will probably rest on the character of Plantagenet Palliser, Lady Glencora, and the Rev. Mr Crawley. [2]

In Australia, at the age of sixty, he had observed that he was getting to be too old to undertake any more trips around the world. He had suffered from a liver complaint and had another hunting accident in which a horse trod on his head. The onset of age was becoming increasingly apparent, and he gave up smoking big cigars, which made him dozy, and eventually settled for smaller ones in his last years. Despite this and other signs of physical slowing, he wrote *Is He Popenjoy?* which he completed just before arriving in Australia. Although not published until 1877/78, it is notable for the satirical account of the 'Female Disabilities' and the ongoing row between the feminists, the American Olivia Q. Fleabody and Baroness Banmann from Bavaria, which is intentionally farcical and has little do with the main plot of inheritance. The novel's analysis of marital stresses is as elsewhere in Trollope, surprisingly modern.

The strands of his life were still various. He had warmed to his friends in Australia, where he was greatly welcomed, and acted decisively with regard to Fred's affairs. His fears were just beneath the surface, and he recorded that he dreaded the arrival of abject old age which would leave him without the ability to do anything. On the way home to England from San Francisco Trollope was on the same boat as Henry James, who found him decent but dull, revising his judgment slightly when he met him later at dinner and found him ordinary but good-humoured. Trollope had completed *The American Senator* two days before arriving in San Francisco: there is yet more hunting in this novel plus the senator's analysis of the English way of life at a public lecture, which leaves him less than popular. Again we are aware that Trollope has deliberately shifted his stance: the criticism of America, indulged in by Frances Trollope and later by Anthony, is here given the reverse twist with England exposed to American scrutiny.

In May 1876 Trollope attended the Lord Mayor's banquet at the Mansion House, and at Christmas Kate Field, having stage commitments in London, came to dinner. He began *The Duke's Children*, the final novel in the political series (it would not be serialized until 1879/80) in which Plantagenet, now Duke of Omnium, has to cope with life without his mainstay, his wife Glencora, whose death is announced at the beginning of the book. The interactions with Americans continue: Plantagenet's son, Lord Silverbridge, marries Isabel Boncassen, an American, against the wishes of his father. In public life still, Trollope spoke at St James's Hall (where Senator Gotobed had delivered his lecture in *The American Senator*) in December 1876 on the vexed Eastern question which divided Russia and Turkey. Trollope was characteristically at odds with Disraeli for his support of the Turks and apparently overran his speaking time, according to an emergent novelist in the audience, Thomas Hardy.

Early in 1877 he began *John Caldigate* (published in *Blackwood's* between1878 and 1879), wrote about his favourite Roman author Cicero in the *Fortnightly* (almost a prelude to his later full treatment of that writer) and then was tempted to travel once more. The Transvaal in South Africa had been occupied by a small force under the control of Sir Theophilus Shepstone, and Trollope determined to go out and see for himself what was happening. He took his decision in May 1877 and set off at the end of June. His underlying motivation may well have been his interest in seeing the condition of the indigenous population, but he was also intent on visiting the Boer states as well as the native homelands and the British areas. His itinerary was to be crowded into less than six months. He spent two weeks in Cape Town, his initial responses conveying the quality of his bias: the city appeared a 'half-bred sort of a place, with an ugly Dutch flavour about it',[3] checked up on the postal system almost from habit, and travelled to meet African chiefs. His sense of humour is shown in a dig at Disraeli, 'In coming ages a Kafir may make as good a Prime Minister as Lord Beaconsfield'.[4] Although Trollope was to write in *South Africa* that it was a country of black men and not of white, he felt that the whites had in fact improved the lot of some of the tribes. He visited Bishop Colenso in Natal, having sympathetic feelings towards him which he had enunciated in his 1866 essay, 'The Clergyman who Subscribes for Colenso'. Colenso had demonstrated that the early books of the Old Testament were not of divine origin and had reaped the whirlwind of stricture as a result.

Trollope's correspondence reflects his ongoing concern for his son Henry, – who was helping Bianconi's daughter write a life of her father, referred to by Anthony as 'your carman's biography' – and he touchingly mentions Rose in this connection by asking Henry if he intends to have his own name on the book as its editor: 'If the book be good I should, and I should take mamma's advice as to the goodness for she is never mistaken about a book being good or bad.'[5]

Naturally, Trollope had contracted to write his own book on the visit as well as providing newspapers with letters, and he did not stint his movements. His interests ranged from ostrich farming to the diamond mines: here Kimberley was the inevitable focus. He found the place 'odious' because of the naked greed which he saw there. Though he regarded work as 'the great civilizer of the world', he observed, 'When I heard of so much a dozen being given to young bairns for the smallest specks of diamonds, specks which their young eyes might possibly discover, my heart was bitterly grieved.'[6] He was similarly critical of the effects of the lure of gold.

By now he weighed more than sixteen stones (with the Banting regime a thing of the past), and his eyes were causing him discomfort, but he was following his inclinations: he was fascinated by the Zulus, and later abridged the fourth edition of his book (1879) while adding a chapter on Zululand as a mark of his disapproval of the Zulu War. Still the regimen of mind and movement, action and writing, continued. The first edition of *South Africa* came out in 1878 and *Is He Popenjoy?* finished its serial run. Another rather different travel excursion followed in June/July 1878 when Trollope went to Iceland with a group of friends on a private yacht. *How the 'Mastiffs' went to Iceland* contains the usual Trollopian spirited observation and entertaining anecdote, as well as some factual reportage: it was privately circulated and has a kind of in-joke flavour about it.

As always he was writing and publishing, but worked on the Copyright Commission and the Royal Literary Fund as well, scrutinizing individual applications for help and investigating them when he could. By now the payments for his novels were falling, almost as if Trollopian goods were a little past their sell-by date, though this did not affect his prodigious output. *Ayala's Angel* was written in this year, though not published until 1881, while *John Caldigate* was enjoying its serial run. Travel both past and present continued to feed into his fiction, for example a story set in Innsbruck called 'Why Frau Frohmann raised her Prices'. But personal sadness was at hand. George Henry Lewes died at the end of November 1878: Trollope celebrated him in an article in the *Fortnightly*, appropriately since Lewes had been the first editor of the magazine. Trollope had loved him, appreciating his talents as raconteur and their good times of literary chat while enjoying a cup of coffee and a cigar. Another short novel, *Cousin Henry*, a morbid tale of wills and deception, was written towards the end of 1878.

In 1878 *An Eye for An Eye*, written some eight years earlier, was at last serialized. It appeared in volume form in the following year, as did *John Caldigate*. The last named makes use of Trollope's Australian experiences and he is also able to bring in his postal expertise about the date issue of a stamp.

A postal official of diligence and deduction called Bagwax is instrumental to the plot: Trollope jokingly identified himself with him by observing, 'Was I not once a Bagwax myself?'[7] Next he hastily cobbled together the subjective book on Thackeray for the new *English Men of Letters* series. Thackeray — like Trollope and George Eliot — had set his face against a biography. Trollope was on good terms with Thackeray's daughter, Anny, who was herself a minor novelist of some repute. Thackeray's other daughter Minny, the first wife of Leslie Stephen (the current editor of the *Cornhill Magazine* and, later, father of Virginia Woolf by his second wife), had died in 1875. It has been rightly argued that Trollope's short book tells us as much about Trollope as it does about Thackeray, since the qualities he praises in Thackeray are often those present in his own writing. Some of Trollope's remarks may have upset Anny, but when they met later things were soon right between them.

In 1880 Trollope's voluminous work on his revered Cicero was published. He had written to his friend G.W. Rusden in 1879 that he had 'an opus magnum for my old age. I am writing a Life of Cicero'.[8] Later he was to notice with a mixture of pride and exhaustion the number of books he had read while compiling the work. It is a major sympathetic study recognized, among others, by the late Enoch Powell, who was himself a classical scholar: he remarked on Trollope's particular ability for describing 'mixed characters, the characters by which he perceived the drama of domestic and political life being played out'.[9] It is typical too that Trollope should give his Latin hero a kind of contemporary currency by suggesting that he would have been very popular at the Carlton Club!

To this time also belongs the radical short novel *Dr Wortle's School*, written in a period of three weeks. How completely engrossed Trollope is can be seen in his bold stroke at the outset. We are led to believe that Dr Wortle's right-hand man Mr Peacocke is a bigamist, and we marvel at the courage and integrity of Dr Wortle in supporting him, defying influential parental opinion, standing up to the innuendoes of the press, and ultimately saving the reputation of his school. The reader feels that there is something of Trollope himself in Wortle – a portrait of the artist as an older man – with his obstinacy, his tenacious clinging to principle and the radical courage of his last years.

Was he aware of the foreshortening of time, of having to cram everything into this last span? Was he tetchy on principle as well? The abridged *South Africa* appeared the same year, with its 'Zululand' chapter: Trollope said of the Zulus in a letter, 'we have already slaughtered 10000 of them, and rejoice in having done so. To me it seems like civilization gone mad!'[10] Elsewhere there are reflexive swipes. He refused to contribute to the Stratford Memorial Theatre venture, for which Kate Field gave her services free.

Certainly, he and his wife were thinking of moving. The London social round was probably exhausting anyway, and in July 1880 they took a house at South Harting close to Petersfield in Sussex: in fact a relative had been the incumbent of South Harting at the end of the eighteenth century. Trollope is reported to have played some part in village affairs – his energies were not yet drained – and there he put the final touches to his *Life of Cicero* (we are told that over this book he fretted about the reviews). Afterwards he began a short novel, *Kept in the Dark*, which was not published until 1882.

On a personal level, he recorded the death of George Eliot. He had been meaning to get in touch with her after their move – and indeed after her marriage to John Walter Cross, twenty years her junior, in May 1880. She died in December: Trollope was shocked by the news. He wrote to Charles Lee Lewes, 'I did love her very dearly',[11] and he told Kate Field that Eliot's personal life should remain private, adding that such privacy should be the lot of all celebrated literary figures.[12] Eliot herself had acknowledged her personal indebtedness to him over *Middlemarch*.

Perhaps this triggered his own brooding consciousness of the sad disabilities of old age, though the creative flow remained unimpaired. Incredibly, in 1882, he produced a novel set nearly a hundred years later, in 1980. The island of Britannula has an appropriately named President Neverbend, who has succeeded in carrying through (and nearly implementing) compulsory euthanasia for each member of the population who reaches the age of sixty-seven. They enter a 'college' at sixty-six by way of preparation before death and cremation, thus avoiding the sufferings of old age. The book was called *The Fixed Period*, its plot loosely deriving from one of the Jacobean plays which Trollope had read – *The Old Law*, by Philip Massinger. The fiction cunningly, if ironically, mirrors its author, who was sixty-seven in 1882. There is no lack of vigour in the writing or in the inventiveness of this mini sci-fi novel which also idiosyncratically anticipates the coming English obsession with cricket. Caricature names like 'Neverbend' do not undermine the focused verve of Trollope as he approached his own 'fixed period'.

Still committed to the Royal Literary Fund and his London friends, he stayed at Garlant's Hotel in Suffolk Street when he had to be in town. He negotiated the sale of *Mr Scarborough's Family* to Charles Dickens Jnr, for serialization in *All the Year Round* (it was running at the time of his death in 1882), but another death certainly affected him. This was of Tom's daughter by his first marriage, Bice, whom Anthony and Rose had cared for at the time of her mother's death. She died after having given birth to a baby girl in July 1881. Still Trollope continued to write in this final phase of his life – a single volume on *Lord Palmerston* in the *English Political Leaders* series, in which he recorded the statesman's career as being one which displayed outstanding courage and integrity. Then a novel with Quakerism at its heart, *Marion Fay*, written between 1878 and 1879, completed its serial run in June 1882. There was still the occasional afternoon of whist at the Athenaeum, and early in 1882 Trollope rejoiced that his son Henry had been elected to membership of that élite club.

During this period he was increasingly troubled by asthma, and undoubtedly by his bulk, which made the climbing of stairs difficult. On one occasion he told Rose somewhat pathetically that he had spent a day being medically examined.[13] He sought reassurance from one of these doctors, a young London man, but was given to morbid reflections from time to time ('it were better that I were dead').[14] He was told to ease up but of course he did not. In the last year of his life he worked at *An Old Man's Love*, that simple tale of renunciation in which the 'old man' Mr Whittlestaff (aged fifty) gives up his love for his ward Mary Lawrie, who is half his age. It was not published until after Trollope's death, in fact in 1884. He also visited Ireland twice during 1882, feeling his age and degrees of fatigue, and working on his uncompleted novel *The Landleaguers*. In a curious way, in his end was his beginning. He was always interested in the state of Ireland question, and now he found the sharp edge of opposition to the Gladstonian policy of Home Rule.

His brother Tom and wife Frances visited Anthony and Rose at Harting in July. Trollope was in the habit of spending more time in the winter at Garlant's Hotel, where he had so often stayed in the past and which must have been something of another home to him. His already bad health was getting worse, and his later letters list a catalogue of ailments which show how much the quality of his life had deteriorated: he could not sleep, he could not write because his hand was paralysed, he could not sit with comfort because he had to wear a truss and, worst of all, asthma plagued him. He complained of great shortage of breath which particularly affected him at night, so that he had to sit up in order to breathe properly. He also had to take chloral.[15] Interestingly, it was Cardinal Newman who had suggested respiratory relief through fumigation for Trollope, who continued to suffer but was undoubtedly pleased that Newman re-read his novels. There is in his final letters a rare pathos, almost as if his independence of action had gone. He reaches out increasingly towards his son Henry: at one stage, at the end of March 1882, he suggests that he and Henry get a small flat for his stays in London.

This did not materialize. On 3 November 1882 he had a stroke and died five weeks later.

CONCLUSION

O f course Trollope lived on through his books, and with the publication of *An Autobiography* in 1883 he presented an image of himself which conditioned appraisals of him through to the end of the century and after. His characteristics were many, various, warm and at times overpowering. Perhaps his outstanding quality was his critical zest for experience which embraced practical life experience and the life of the imagination, both being charged with his abundant and remarkable energy. He worked hard, he wrote hard, he played hard. A conservative who loved the good things of life, he was also a radical who queried their abuse. Robustly English, he was yet gifted with a world-awareness which traversed the present and looked to the future. He loved engaging with people and he created people; he hated corruption, and attacked it uncompromisingly in an age which witnessed gigantic swindles. He created his people with a compassionate insight into their limitations without condescension; he loved tradition and an ordered and moral way of life, but he was receptive to change.

That heavily bearded face looking out from faded photographs tells us little or nothing: that heavily selective *An Autobiography* tells us a little more but not much. Sir William Gregory, Trollope's contemporary at Harrow who later introduced him to men of letters and people of some substance in Irish society, found him the dirtiest and most unkempt boy he had ever come across but nonetheless rather liked him. Justin McCarthy, who saw Trollope under cross-examination in the court house in Tralee in 1849, was impressed by his good humour despite his reputation for being overbearing and bad-tempered. He also had a reputation for terrifying those who were responsible to him in the Post Office, and the foregoing account contains examples of his being in conflict with his superiors and of being found awkward, difficult and obtuse as a result. There is the story of Trollope's impetuosity, his on-the-spot reaction without thinking when he is alleged to have said, 'I differ from you entirely! What was it you said?'[1] There is G. A. Sala's recollection of Trollope being able to fall asleep at any moment, whether standing up or not; to Dickens at one time he was ' a perfect cordial'; [2] to Wilkie Collins he had the effect of a gale; and to W. Lucas Collins, a regular contributor to *Blackwoods* and editor of *Ancient Classics for Modern Readers*, he was a personal friend, a genial and loving man who was always performing little kindnesses. These are outward appraisals and, since his own reticence about his private life requires deduction from the few clues, it is by his published writing and through his letters that we best know the man. The range of his interests, his dedication as a public servant and, despite his tendency to rush into print, a pride in himself as a professional writer, these and many other qualities endear him to us. There are paradoxes, particular biases and contradictions, and they were present in Trollope. But there is in him too a kind of integrity, a forthrightness, in his fiction, in his letters, in his public conduct: more than that, there is a trenchant independence of viewpoint which is refreshing and revealing. The term 'political correctness' could not be applied to him, since he forged his own way regardless of convention. This accounts for the antipathy he aroused in some – like Sir Rowland Hill – and the disgust he felt at the corruptions in the society which he saw around him.

The veil of reticence in *An Autobiography* is never lowered. In its final pages Trollope refers to the book as 'this so-called autobiography'[3] and says that he has had no intention of revealing his inner life. Reading his fiction and travel today, and with some knowledge of his career dedication, love of family and work on behalf of others, we know something of that inner life through what he wrote and did. When Augustus Melmotte, the degraded financier, swindler and Member of Parliament for Westminster, kills himself in drunken loneliness with prussic acid in *The Way We Live Now* Trollope, who has exposed him completely, somehow contrives a sympathetic identification with him which moves the reader to pity despite Melmotte's crimes. It shows the nature of Trollope's own humanity, his capacity to enter the man's mind at the end and convey the abject desolation, the terminal nullity of his taking his life. Trollope's inwardness is this sympathetic capacity: his outwardness is shown in another way, but it is interactive with the inwardness in terms of imagination and feeling.

Here he is conveying an experience which would perhaps be shared by many twentieth-century travellers, but the uniqueness of the account derives from the uniqueness of the individual who wrote it:

> That which at first was only great and beautiful, becomes gigantic and sublime till the mind is at a loss to find an epithet for its own use. To realize Niagara you must sit there till you see nothing else than that which you have come to see. You will hear nothing else, and think of nothing else. At length you will be at one with the tumbling river before you. You will find yourself among the waters as though you belonged to them. The cool liquid green will run through your veins, and the voice of the cataract will be the expression of your own heart. You will fall as the bright waters fall, rushing down into your new world with no hesitation and no dismay; and you will rise again as the spray rises, bright, beautiful, and pure. Then you will flow away in your course to the uncompassed, distant, and eternal ocean.[4]

These seem fitting words with which to close this brief life of a major writer who at one and the same time mirrored his age yet transcended it by the enquiring independence of his stance about many aspects of the Victorian era. He recorded what he saw with a keen appraisal that was warm either with appreciation or criticism, and he created in his creatures the tribulations and happiness – the darkness and the irradiations – of the human condition. It has been noted by others that Trollope is not highly favoured in academic circles in this country, that he does not often appear on university syllabuses, though it is certainly true that scholars and critics find him important enough to write about. Perhaps it is that he is not intellectual or philosophical in the strict definitions of that term, that he exemplifies what Henry James singled out as the ordinary rather than the exceptional. Like his friend George Eliot he had to wait for the passing of a century before he was admitted to Westminster Abbey: like her, he spoke to the heart, for his own was large both in the practical actions of life and in the imagined but nonetheless real actions of fiction.

NOTES AND
REFERENCES

INTRODUCTION

1. Anthony Trollope, *An Autobiography* (Edinburgh and London, William Blackwood & Sons,1883), 2nd edn, vol I, p. viii. (Hereafter *AA* followed by vol, chapter and page number).
2. R.H. Super, *The Chronicler of Barsetshire: A Life of Anthony Trollope* (Ann Arbor, University of Michigan Press, 1988), p. viii. (Hereafter Super followed by page number).

CHAPTER ONE

1. *The Letters of Anthony Trollope*, edited by N. John Hall, (2 vols, Stanford University Press, 1983), I, p. 2. (Hereafter *L* followed by volume and page number).
2. Super, p. 11.
3. *AA*, I. ii, p. 33.
4. *AA*, I. ii, p. 42.
5. *AA*, I. i, p. 6.
6. Anthony Trollope, *The Three Clerks* (1858), ch. xxvii.
7. *AA*, I. ii, p. 32.
8. *AA*, I. iii, pp. 62–3.

CHAPTER TWO

1. *AA*, I. iii, pp. 57–8.
2. *AA*, I. iv, p. 91.
3. *AA*, I. iv, pp. 94–5.
4. *L* I. p. 24, footnote 6.
5. *AA*, I. v, p. 123.
6. R.H. Super, *Trollope in the Post Office* (Michigan, 1981), p. 22.

7. *L*, I, p. 28.
8. Ibid.
9. *AA*, I. v, p. 131.
10. *L*, I, p. 46.

CHAPTER THREE

1. *AA*, I. ii, p. 44.
2. *L* I, p. 64.
3. Super, p. 88.
4. Anthony Trollope, *The West Indies and the Spanish Main* (1859), Chapter 1 – Introductory.
5. *The Letters of Mrs Gaskell*, edited by J.A.V. Chapple and Arthur Pollard (Manchester University Press, 1966), p. 602.
6. *AA*, II. xvii, pp. 158–9.
7. *L* I, p. 144.
8. Quoted in Super, p. 142.
9. Richard Mullen, *Anthony Trollope: A Victorian in his World* (London, Duckworth, 1990), p. 411. (Hereafter Mullen).

CHAPTER FOUR

1. *L* I, p. 238.
2. Anthony Trollope, *Thackeray* (1879), p. 60.
3. Henry James in the *Nation*, 28 September 1865.
4. Anthony Trollope, *Can You Forgive Her?* (1864–5), ch. xlv.
5. *Pall Mall Gazette*, 21 April 1866, p. 12.
6. Anthony Trollope, *The Fixed Period* (1882), ch. ix.
7. *AA*, I. x, p. 234.
8. *AA*, II. xv, pp. 108–9.
9. Elizabeth R. Epperly, *Anthony Trollope's Notes on the Old Drama* (BC, Canada, University of Victoria, 1988), p. 13.
10. *L* I, p. 433.
11. *L* I, p. 429.

CHAPTER FIVE

1. *AA*, II. xvi, p. 128.
2. *AA*, II. xvi, p. 134.

3. *AA*, II. xvi, pp. 134–5.
4. *AA*, II. xvi, p. 141.
5. Anthony Trollope, *The Vicar of Bullhampton* (1870), preface.
6. *AA*, II. xviii, p. 182.
7. *St Paul's Magazine*, July 1870.
8. Robert Polhemus, *The Changing World of Anthony Trollope* (Berkeley, University of California Press, 1968).
9. T.H.S. Escott, *Anthony Trollope: His Work, Associates and Literary Originals* (1913), p. 280.
10. *AA*, II. xix, p. 193.
11. *AA*, II. xix, p. 194.
12. Mullen, p. 535.
13. Anthony Trollope, *Lady Anna* (1873), ch. xlviii.
14. *L*, II, p. 561.
15. *L*, II, p. 557.
16. *The George Eliot Letters*, edited by Gordon S. Haight (9 vols 1954–78, Yale), vol. V, p. 357. (G.H. Lewes Diary, 1 January 1873).
17. *AA*, II. xx, p. 211.

CHAPTER SIX

1. *The Tireless Traveller: Twenty Letters to the Liverpool Mercury by Anthony Trollope, 1875*, edited by Bradford Booth (California, 1941; reprinted 1978), p. 217.
2. *AA*, II. xx, pp. 219–20.
3. *L*, II, p. 731.
4. Quoted by Super, p. 371.
5. *L*, II, p. 739.
6. Anthony Trollope, *South Africa* (1878), vol, II, ch. ix.
7. *L*, II, p. 815.
8. *L*, II, p. 842.
9. *Trollopiana* 21 (May 1993), 12.
10. *L*, II, p. 826.
11. *L*, II, p. 887.
12. *L*, II, p. 892.
13. *L*, II, p. 955.
14. *L*, II, p. 936.

15. *L*, II, p. 993.

CONCLUSION

1. Quoted in R.C. Terry (ed.), *Trollope: Interviews and Recollections* (London, Macmillan, 1987), p. 51.
2. Ibid, p. 127.
3. *AA*, II, xx, p. 225.
4. Anthony Trollope, *North America* (1862), vol I, ch. vii.

BIBLIOGRAPHY

COLLECTED EDITIONS

Oxford University Press (World's Classics) printed all Trollope's fiction in this series, with the stories in two volumes — *The Early Stories* and *The Later Stories* — with introductions and annotations. A fine hardback edition of the *Collected Shorter Fiction* (edited by Julian Thompson) was published by Robinson (London) in 1992. Penguin Books issued all the fiction (unannotated) early in the 1990s. The Trollope Society has virtually completed its hardback edition of the fiction, including the five volumes of stories. The travel books and many of the novels were issued by Sutton in paperback in the late 1980s, but did not include *New Zealand*. Trollope's *An Autobiography* (Oxford University Press, 1980), edited by P.D. Edwards, is available in World's Classics.

BIOGRAPHIES, STUDIES, LETTERS

There is a Trollope industry, and the selection below has been kept brief deliberately to focus readers on particular areas.

Edwards, P.D., *Anthony Trollope: His Art and Scope* (Hassocks, Harvester Press, 1978).

Glendinning, Victoria, *Trollope* (London, Hutchinson, 1992).

Hall, N. John, *Trollope: A Biography* (Oxford, Clarendon Press, 1991).

Bibliography

Hall, N. John (ed.), *The Letters of Anthony Trollope*, 2 vols. (Stanford University Press, 1983).

Hall, N. John, *Trollope and His Illustrators* (London, Macmillan, 1980).

Hamer, Mary, *Writing by Numbers: Trollope's Serial Fiction* (Cambridge University Press, 1987).

Handley, Graham (ed.), *Trollope the Traveller: Selections from Anthony Trollope's Travel Writings* (London, Pickering & Chatto, 1993).

Mullen, Richard, *Anthony Trollope: A Victorian in His World* (London, Duckworth, 1990).

Mullen, Richard, with Munson, James, *The Penguin Companion to Trollope* (London, Penguin Books, 1996).

Overton, Bill, *The Unofficial Trollope* (Brighton, Harvester Press, 1982).

Skilton, David, *Anthony Trollope and His Contemporaries* (London, Longman, 1972; reprinted Basingstoke, Macmillan, 1996).

Smalley, Donald (ed.), *Trollope: The Critical Heritage* (London, Routledge & Kegan Paul, 1969; pbk edn, 1985; London, Routledge, 1995).

Super, R.H., *The Chronicler of Barsetshire: A Life of Anthony Trollope* (Ann Arbor, Michigan University Press, 1988).

Super, R.H., *Trollope in the Post Office* (Ann Arbor, University of Michigan Press, 1981).

Terry, R.C., *Anthony Trollope: The Artist in Hiding* (London, Macmillan, 1977).

Terry, R.C., (ed.), *Trollope: Interviews and Recollections* (Basingstoke, Macmillan, 1987).

Terry, R.C., (ed.), *The Oxford Reader's Companion to Anthony*

Trollope (Oxford University Press, 1999).

Tracy, Robert, *Trollope's Later Novels* (Berkeley, University of California Press, 1978).

Wall, Stephen, *Trollope and Character* (London, Faber & Faber, 1988).

POCKET BIOGRAPHIES

For a copy of our complete list or details of other Sutton titles, please contact Emma Leitch at Sutton Publishing Limited, Phoenix Mill, Thrupp, Stroud, Gloucestershire, GL5 2BU

POCKET BIOGRAPHIES

Christopher Wren
James Chambers

Che Guevara
Andrew Sinclair

W.G. Grace
Donald Trelford

The Brontës
Kathryn White

Lawrence of Arabia
Jeremy Wilson

Christopher Columbus
Peter Riviere

Martin Luther King
Harry Harmer

Genghis Khan
James Chambers

James Dean
William Hall

Cleopatra
E.E. Rice

John Ruskin
Francis O'Gorman

Joseph Stalin
Harold Shukman

Juan and Eva Perón
Clive Foss

Queen Victoria
Elizabeth Longford

Anthony Trollope
Graham Handley

For a copy of our complete list or details of other Sutton titles, please contact Emma Leitch at Sutton Publishing Limited, Phoenix Mill, Thrupp, Stroud, Gloucestershire, GL5 2BU

POCKET BIOGRAPHIES

FORTHCOMING

Byron
Catherine Peters

J.B. Priestley
Dulcie Gray

Fidel Castro
Clive Foss

For a copy of our complete list or details of other Sutton titles, please contact Emma Leitch at Sutton Publishing Limited, Phoenix Mill, Thrupp, Stroud, Gloucestershire, GL5 2BU